Presenting the Past

Presenting the Past

Psychoanalysis and the Sociology of Misremembering

Jeffrey Prager

HARVARD UNIVERSITY PRESS

Cambridge, Massachusetts, and London, England, 1998

Library of Congress Cataloging-in-Publication Data

Prager, Jeffrey, 1948–
    Presenting the past : psychoanalysis and the sociology of
misremembering / Jeffrey Prager.
      p. cm.
    Includes bibliographical references and index.
    ISBN 0-674-56641-6 (alk. paper)
    1. Psychoanalysis and culture.   2. Memory.
3. Memory—Case studies.   4. False memory syndrome.
5. False memory syndrome—Case studies.   I. Title.
BF175.4.C84P73   1998
153.1′2—dc21   97-49904

For Debby and Daniel, all of me

Contents

Presenting the Past

Introduction

I am a sociologist, and several years ago I undertook a full clinical training in psychoanalysis. My purpose in pursuing this training was to bring the knowledge and insights of psychoanalysis to bear on my sociological research interests. Over the years, those interests have focused on various belief systems or ideologies and their social expression. I have explored how particular social structures, politics, and cultures influence those belief systems and, just as important, how the belief systems shape the societies from which they spring. I have studied nationalist movements, for example, and also American racism. At the time of my analytic training, I had long been convinced that my sociological work could benefit from more robust and developed theories of the self, of the individual personality, of subjectivity, and of the unconscious. Psychoanalysis offered the possibility of a sustained encounter with these dimensions of personal and social life.

Psychoanalytic training is premised on the bridging of theory and practice: in addition to seminars in psychoanalytic scholarship, it requires one to undergo analysis oneself, and to conduct the analysis of others, under the supervision of senior analysts. In-depth encounters with individual selves—my own and others—promised to be especially instructive. I hoped the practice of psychoanalysis would enrich my theory of ideology and belief systems by enabling me to better comprehend the relation between personal convictions and the social and cultural worlds that helped generate them.

But the training instead made me increasingly aware of the difficulty of generalizing from the individual to the social whole. Through my clinical work I came to understand individual uniqueness and idiosyncrasy and to appreciate the great challenge of attempting to enter another person's system of meaning and signification. It seemed that "doing sociology" and "doing psychoanalysis," rather than being complementary or even compatible endeavors, were taking me in opposing directions.

I became especially disenchanted with efforts—for example, in attitude or survey research—to comprehend individual motivation and personal conviction through the use of large-scale aggregate data and the language of statistical probabilities and tendencies. And yet I believed that such research described an important social reality that was overlooked by psychoanalysis: social science discovers impersonal and broadly based social forces that affect both the life experience and the understandings of individuals and collectivities. I hoped to find common ground between the social scientific move toward the impersonal and aggregate and the psychoanalytic interest in the individual and idiosyncratic.

I was struck by certain common epistemological assumptions that unified the two. Social science is committed to an inductive, data-driven approach to the accumulation of knowledge, and to minimizing the impact on research of the scientist's preconceived notions and prejudices. The presenting world, not the observer of it, is given pride of place in social scientific inquiry. Similarly, a good psychoanalyst is able to suspend certainty about the connections between one's experience and one's feelings and convictions, so as to enter into another person's system of mapping meanings. Any effort to make these connections on the basis of some external standard of logic or rationality is just as likely to be wrong for any given individual as it is to be right. The suspension of personal biases or presuppositions in favor of the evidence as it presents itself is a critical feature of both social science and psychoanalysis.

But at my most psychoanalytic I came to believe that genuine communication and understanding could be achieved only in a psychoanalytic setting (and there only rarely). Finding a way to connect psychoanalytic findings with sociological ones seemed more difficult than ever. While I still believed that nationalist ideologies or racist beliefs, for example, transcend individuals and are of great social import, I despaired of the possibility of delineating a natural history of these phenomena: one person's racial attitudes, let us say, and the meaning they hold for that person, cannot stand in for another person's racial attitudes and their meaning to that other person. The social expression of belief systems and the personal functions they serve do not calibrate as neatly as I had imagined they would.

But over time I began to see ways in which the individual and social interpenetrate. In my analytic practice I was confronting individual patients who came to treatment because of various kinds of life crises and who, through analysis, were attempting to understand their unhappiness, their inability to make decisions, their feelings of being unfulfilled, and other unpleasant states of being. They were trying to understand how both past experiences and feelings and current self-perceptions contributed to their dissatisfaction. What became striking was that they used "categories of experience" made available by the culture, what we might call frames of meaning, to understand the sources of their troubles. For example, a patient who was unhappily married raised the question of sexual orientation as a possible source of his distress: could it be, he wondered, that he was homosexual? Then there was a patient who, through her analysis, came to recognize the importance of her experiences as an African American for her feelings about herself, and for her relations to others. Another patient wondered whether her difficulty in developing satisfying relationships as an adult could possibly have been caused by abuse in her childhood.

Patients invoke such categories—homosexual, African American, abused—to capture profound and significant dimensions of themselves, elements of being that are outside their volition or choice. The categories are often accompanied by elaborated narratives of experience, in which personal history is interwoven with tales of suffering that include themes of estrangement or discrimination, recognition or redemption. These narrative elements that connect the category to a larger story are not solely of the individual's own making, but reflect substantial borrowing from a culture that has perfected various tales of victimization. In appropriating a category, one often takes the first step in situating oneself in a whole story of one's past, linking past experiences to one's present-day distress. But while the categories are employed for personal aims, they are fundamentally cultural: frames of experience that are presented from the outside, organized by the society as meaningful features of the lives of its members. They offer a connection to the nameless, faceless numbers who were abused, or homosexual, or African American, a connection through which one can understand oneself and orient oneself in relation to others.[1]

These categories, and their use in narrative, reveal not merely individual subjectivity but also the individual's participation in the culture. In appropriating a particular tale of a past, an individual simultaneously connects himself or herself to a particular kind of living in the present. Psychoanalytic patients naturally take cues from the outside world and apply them to their own circumstances: does this fit my experience? does this explain me? It becomes nearly impossible to parse out memories of the past from the categories of experience available in the present, the narratives offered to link the present to a story of its origins in the past, and the consequences of these particular forms of self-understanding for the rememberer in the present.

It is not uncommon for a person who has appropriated particular frames of meaning to seek out groups that confirm those frames of meaning. Someone might begin to attend a group for adult survivors of incest, or join an organization celebrating racial distinctiveness, or even engage in homosexual activity on the basis of these understandings. And while the affirmation one receives from "finding oneself" may be gratifying, the relation between self-understanding and social experience is murky. Does experience drive self-understanding? Or is it the other way around?

These questions arise at the intersection of the personal

and the social. Patients do not only run through the various available categories of explanation. In the psychoanalytic consulting room or perhaps before they walk in, they try on for size their own theory of what caused their unhappiness, exploring its explanatory power and its usefulness for restructuring their lives. And the patient isn't the only one in the room engaged in that kind of work. So is the analyst. The analyst is no less involved with the cultural categories of significance in attempting to organize the patients' life experiences, to understand their current symptoms, or to explain them to themselves. An analyst's thinking about patients is as culturally embedded as is their thinking about themselves. Analysts experience and relate to people differently according to cultural categories: man or woman, young or old, black or white, Jew or Gentile. These categories express profound and elaborate cultural understandings: the phenomenal world of experience is always mediated through the cultural representations by which experience is organized, framed, and narrated.

What distinguishes analysts from patients, one might say, is the analysts' greater experience with the unconscious and their training to tolerate and to understand the nonrational, the illogical, the ways in which past and present occupy the same psychic space, how otherwise mature adults continue to experience the world through the lenses of childhood, and how the worlds of fantasy and reality interpenetrate in everyone. Analysts bring to the treatment what they have learned about the unconscious (itself a cultural category) and an understanding that their role is to help patients discover the significant role it plays in life. It might also be said that the analyst's task is to demonstrate that the unconscious is first among equals with these cultural categories: the patterns of belief and affect lodged in a person's unconscious drive experience more profoundly than gender, age, race, or other categories of what might be called "external reality."

That lesson is an important one for the patient, and it also serves to remind the analyst to resist an all-too-easy reliance on these external categories. As the psychoanalyst Jacob Arlow has said, "the really significant part of the analytic situation is the concentration of attention on the process of introspection, that is, the creation of a set of conditions that minimize the contribution of the external world and enhance the emergence of derivatives of the inner world—the world of fantasy thinking."[2] It has been argued that this is what the analyst contributes to the analytic process. Indeed, this sustained investigation of the unconscious is the most profound and significant cultural contribution of psychoanalysis.

This is not to say that the involvement between analyst and patient concerns only the discovery of the unconscious. Nor is it to imply that cultural categories are irrelevant to the analyst, bound as he or she is to what might be called commonsense knowledge. Communication in analysis is more than communication about the unconscious, as important as that is. The analyst is naturally engaged with the patient's recollections and descriptions of life's experiences, and together they distinguish between the relevant and irrelevant features that shape unconscious experience. Together they develop a narrative account of the patient's life, focusing on features that were especially important in shaping current experience and feeling.

In this endeavor, both are dependent upon the patient's

recollections. The inequality between the two parties is most evident here; the analyst waits as memories are produced (or not) by the patient. The challenge to the analyst in allowing unconscious thought and remembering to surface is to avoid automatic or premature acceptance of the narrative forms offered by the patient, which may be defenses created to ward off painful affect. But of course not all experience is defensive; it can also be formative and determinative. How does one distinguish between tales of abandonment, estrangement, abuse, discrimination, humiliation, shame, or trauma that shape affect, belief, relationships, and behavior, and those narratives designed to inhibit exploration of the unconscious? Arlow describes well the interaction that occurs in the search for self-understanding:

> The joint search by patient and analyst for the picture of the patient's past is a reciprocal process. In a sense, we dream along with our patients, supplying at first data from our own store of images in order to objectify the patient's memory into some sort of picture. We then furnish this picture to the analysand who responds with further memories, associations, and fantasies; that is, we stimulate him to respond with a picture of his own.[3]

Arlow presents the external world as of diminishing importance to the work of psychoanalysis, and indeed, this preoccupation with an individual's unconscious remains a normative orientation in analytic treatment. The psychoanalyst Sanford Abend points out that patients enter psychoanalysis with a particular fantasy, usually unconscious, of how they will be cured. The analyst harbors similar unconscious fantasies, though probably different from one patient to the next, about how cure can be achieved. Abend argues that such fantasies—for both analyst and patient—derive from "unconscious wishes for the fulfillment of childhood libidinal desires," and that the encounter between the analyst and the patient is thus profoundly subjective. A fantasy of cure implies, too, an assumption—either conscious or unconscious—of the presence of illness.[4]

These theories of illness and its origins, while informed by unconscious desires of both analyst and patient, cannot be understood without reference to a cultural framework. Analytic work is profoundly bounded by culture, and through culturally instilled beliefs about what experiences are meaningful and significant—what needs to be remembered and what can be forgotten—the social is necessarily infused into this very personal self-exploration. It is naive to imagine that the psychoanalytic setting can escape the frame of assumptions about self and society, about past and present, about fantasy and reality, that produced the setting in the first place.

This permeability between the self and the social world, and the difficulty in distinguishing between the two, crystallized for me in one particular case. That case is the focus of this book. The patient was a woman whom I will call Ms. A., who in the course of her psychoanalysis came to believe that her father had sexually abused her when she was very young. As this belief intensified, she found it increasingly difficult to function in her day-to-day life. She had long prided herself on her skill in both personal and professional dealings, but she now found these abilities diminishing dramatically. She confronted her father with her charges of abuse, broke off relations with other family members, and became more and more insistent that I corroborate her beliefs. She wanted me to give her permission to attend a group designed to aid adult survivors of childhood incest, and she demanded that I read the literature on the treatment of adults who had been sexually abused in childhood.

For my part, I was quite surprised to hear of Ms. A.'s suspicions. Little in the preceding year and a half of treatment had prepared me for this direction in our work together. And having heard only her assertion that she had been abused, unsupported by any specific recollections of incidents of abuse, I found myself unpersuaded, and neither granted her permission nor forbade her to attend a survivors' group. At the same time, I was not confident in my own skepticism about her memories. I wavered between feeling that my uncertainty sprang from my professional integrity, which demanded that "truth prevail," and worrying that I was discovering the limits of my capacity to empathize with a woman's experience.

By the end of the analysis, Ms. A.'s views had changed and her demands for corroboration had substantially lessened. She no longer maintained that the abuse had occurred, and, moreover, she believed that the "memories" had been products of current psychic conflicts both with me and with her father. "Remembering" trauma, she concluded, had been her unconscious attempt to defend against painful, embarrassing, and seemingly dangerous emotions. Recalling her father as evil, she came to believe, had been a defensive denial of strong positive feelings toward him that had recently resurfaced.

There are various ways to understand this shift in

Ms. A.'s memories, and I will consider alternative explanations, including the possibility that she simply complied
with my own reservations. But whatever its causes, there
is no denying that Ms. A.'s experience demonstrates the
malleability of memory. Ms. A. entered analytic treatment
with particular understandings and expectations—some
well formed, others more inchoate—about the historical
origins of her current unhappiness and the route to a cure.
In the analysis she produced substantial memories of early
experiences and feelings that supported those recollections. Later, her comprehension of the relation of her present to her past shifted, as she considered the possibility that
she had been sexually abused. Now the kinds of memories
she was searching for similarly shifted; her recollection of
the past was coming to serve different purposes and to
assume distinctive coloration. Toward the end of the analysis, yet another change yielded yet another set of memories, coupled with a new relation to her past and to those
significant to her in the present.

My task in this book is to investigate this process of shifting memories. I intend not merely to document the malleability of memory, an aim that aligns this work with other
contemporary research about remembering. In addition,
by bringing together insights from sociology and psychoanalysis, I hope to give meaning to that malleability. The
question of why memories shift over time has been the
object of little sustained investigation.

By the end of treatment Ms. A. recognized that memory
was as much a product of the present as of the past: recollections were influenced by her present-day relationships, both with her family members and with me, her
analyst. Together we concluded that her psychoanalysis

demonstrated that the past continues to serve the present: that we use what we remember or construct of the past to protect ourselves from or to give meaning to our affective needs and desires in our present relationships, especially intimate ones.

Beyond that, I was deeply impressed by the ways in which the outside world penetrated the inner world of meaning and experience. My analytic work with Ms. A. focused on discovering her individual mind—drawing out feelings, thoughts, experiences, unconscious beliefs, and fantasies—leaving behind, if you will, the material or external world. Analysis, in large measure, is about peeling away externals to discover the workings of the unconscious and the effects on it of past experiences and earlier relationships. But suddenly, with the onset of Ms. A.'s memories of abuse, I found myself embroiled, along with my patient, in contemporary controversies about sexual abuse and traumatic experiences in childhood. We entered, via this very personal path, the social world of "adult survivor groups," "repressed memory," "childhood trauma," and other themes that connected us with these broader cultural currents and that threatened to overwhelm the analysis.

When Ms. A. reported her conviction that she had recovered a memory of sexual abuse by her father, there had not yet developed in the culture a counter-reaction to the "recovered memory movement," or any sustained accusations that therapists or popular literature might be responsible for such recollections. It was a time of growing awareness of the prevalence of childhood incest, often covered up by family members complicit in the crime. It was also a time of increasing attention to alleged satanic cults that were said to promote horrific forms of child abuse.

While this "new reality" was being uncovered through startling revelations in the media, Ms. A., like thousands of others, was attempting through the therapeutic process to understand her own unhappiness. In the cultural environment of the time it was inevitable that she would consider early childhood abuse as a possible source of her difficulties, that she would wonder whether long-forgotten traumatic experiences might be the key that would unlock the true cause of her problems. At the very least, such a possibility—while horrible—might promise a close to the seemingly endless search for self-understanding. Just as important, it offered the hope that external trauma, not internal fantasy, was the cause of her personal crisis. Indeed, I believe that this propensity to locate responsibility outside oneself—in the world beyond individual actions or complicity—characterizes our current cultural moment. Ascribing personal unhappiness to trauma and abuse is only one expression of this broader attempt to externalize pain, and, as I will argue in Chapter 4, to desubjectivize it.

In response to this rupture in the psychoanalytic dyad of Ms. A. and myself—her recollections, my skepticism— my sociological voice reemerged, now suffused with an appreciation of the ways in which individuals appropriate the social for their own purposes. My subjective response to Ms. A.'s memories, while instinctive and interpersonal, also reflected the fact that I was deeply steeped in a sociological sensibility, sensitive to the ways in which ways of being are socially constructed. Ms. A. was struggling to determine whether the trope of abuse could promote her own happiness: could seeing herself as an "adult survivor" serve her positively in the present? I, in turn, felt there was an imperfect match between these strong cultural currents, to which both of us were susceptible, and the difficulties interfering with Ms. A.'s happiness. As I was thinking about memory and the purposes to which it is put in the present, my training in sociology helped buttress my response to Ms. A.'s claims, providing me with reason to believe that my reaction to her memories was a consequence of the relationship we had developed and not an unthinking and defensive reaction to her trauma and to its putative recollection.

This book took shape, then, as my attempt to explain the nature of the intersubjective communication between Ms. A. and me and to understand the rupture between us around the twin issues of trauma and incest. But, more broadly, I conceived the book as a way to use this moment in a psychoanalytic treatment to explore the complicated relation between the individual and the collective, and the ways in which the cultural interpenetrates the most individual of pursuits, memory and self-constitution, and the most personal of relationships, that between analyst and patient.

In the subsequent chapters, I will explore memory formation and elaboration from these different vantage points, all with an eye to expanding upon the important insight that memory of the past and the present in which the remembering occurs cannot be neatly disentangled. In Chapter 1 I will provide a detailed report of my work with Ms. A., and I will demonstrate the connection between the production of memories and interpersonal relationships. In Chapter 2 I will explore the current debate about memory, focusing on the repressed memory controversy, and will argue against the idea that remembering can be separated from the social world in which it happens. In Chapter 3 I will present my own theory of memory, calling on my training as both a sociologist and a psychoanalyst, and will locate the process of remembering at the intersection of an individual rememberer and his or her present-day inter-personal and social world. In promoting an intersubjective conception of memory, I challenge those who claim that the key to understanding the phenomenon of recovered memory lies either within the brain itself or within the past itself—claims that isolate memory from the social world in which remembering is embedded.

In the final two chapters I will consider the ways in which this conception of memory as isolated has become institutionalized. In Chapter 4 I will look at the history of psychoanalysis, at Freud's own struggle against a concept of psychic pain as externally caused and his movement toward a concept of it as internally determined—by what he described as psychic reality. I will note the powerful tendency within psychiatry to offer an external theory of psychic pain. This tendency, which I call an attack on sub-jectivity, is characterized by an effort to replace an elabo-rated conception of individual psychology with an objec-tivist, biological, and antivolitional model of the human being.

In Chapter 5 I will turn to the state of our understanding of memory, particularly as expressed by brain researchers and neuroscientists. Here, too, there is a presumption that the "isolated brain" functions independently of interper-sonal and social context. The result is that memory—a brain function—is understood as an objective process. This conception enabled Ms. A., for example, to believe that the memories she "recovered" were a true record of the past and to ignore the ways in which her remembering was an expression of her interpersonal relations in the present.

I believe that these dominant views of memory—now institutionalized within psychiatry and neuroscience— contributed to Ms. A.'s recollection of abuse in her early childhood. I offer an intersubjective alternative to the dominant views. I advance this in the spirit of appreciating both the subjectivity and the sociality of the individual. It is a conception that grants the present a central place in our unending efforts to situate ourselves in relation to our pasts. It also recognizes the complexity of the individual subject, and as such it speaks for the merits of the psychoanalytic method of exploring the nature of the self.

1

Ms. A. and the Problem of Misremembering

Ms. A. sought therapy shortly after arriving in Los Angeles to pursue a highly demanding advanced degree.[1] She had graduated from an excellent eastern university near her home town and then moved west to begin her graduate studies. She was referred to me by an analyst who knew that I was in the early stages of my training and consequently would accept patients for reduced fees.

Ms. A. was an attractive, well-dressed, and well-spoken young woman. Describing her reasons for seeking therapy, she told of experiencing a vast chasm between the way she presented herself to and was perceived by the outside world and the way she felt inside. Other people saw her as supremely competent, effortlessly managing a demanding personal and academic life. She had also overcome many personal disappointments and profound losses. But she felt overwhelmed by others' expectations of her and was constantly sad, often spending her time alone in tears. She thought of herself as unattractive and somewhat overweight, and she was unsure about her femininity. She hoped therapy would close this gap between her inner and outer worlds: she aspired to be able both to reveal her feelings to others and to take pleasure in her accomplishments and her friendships. She was determined to avail herself of therapy—indeed, to dedicate herself to it—so that the painfulness of her subjective experiences would not persist throughout her life.

Ms. A. was the youngest child in a large urban, working-class, and religiously devout family. Both her parents were very active in a fundamentalist Christian religious movement. Her mother, in particular, demanded devotion from all her children and frequently chastised them for not being pious enough. This religious atmosphere permeated interactions between the children and their parents, but there was another important element: the father was an alcoholic. At times he was loud and verbally abusive, but more often he simply withdrew; Ms. A.'s memories of him were predominantly of his absence. This isolation from the family was partly his own choice but also the result of his wife's insistence that he be ostracized. For her he was an object of condemnation and ridicule, the means by which she underscored her special place in the family as the upholder of religious values.

As Ms. A. remembers it, her father's alcoholism grew more severe as the years went by, and was at its worst after the older children had left home, when Ms. A. was living alone with her parents. During those years the conflicts between her parents were especially intense, and she often wondered whether they would remain together and, if not, what would become of her. Her mother instructed her not to discuss her father's problem with anyone, including her older siblings. It was to be treated as their secret, a source of shame and embarrassment no one else should know about, not even other family members.

In earlier years, while her older brothers and sisters were still at home, Ms. A. developed a very close, symbiotic relationship with her mother. Her mother readily admitted that Ms. A. was her favorite, the one most like her. In return, Ms. A. came to feel and say exactly what she imagined her mother wanted her to feel or say. She was very compliant, with an intense religiosity and a hostile and negative attitude toward those of whom her mother disapproved. She also avoided any behavior that would make her seem young or feminine, apparently in an effort to preserve her special place with her mother by imitating her exactly. Her feelings toward her father similarly mirrored her mother's. She was disdainful of him and disgusted with his alcoholism, and she actively endorsed her mother's desire to keep his condition secret from the rest of the world.

And yet, from the age of seven or eight, Ms. A. engaged in various forms of substance abuse. With her older siblings as her suppliers, she began to drink heavily and to smoke both cigarettes and marijuana. She recalled watching her adolescent siblings and their friends experiment sexually and with drugs. She also remembered their pleasure when their little sister would sample tobacco, drugs, and alcohol. From this young age the split developed between the compliant "little adult"—like her mother—and the secretive, naughty girl. How much of her motivation was simply to numb psychic pain and how much to rebelliously assert her independence is difficult to know. But substance abuse continued throughout her adolescence. In her early twenties, after leaving home and after experiencing difficulties with personal relationships, Ms. A. came to see herself as an alcoholic. She suffered, like her father, from periodic blackouts, and during one of them she was involved in an automobile accident. After that she began attending Alcoholics Anonymous. When she entered analysis she had been a devoted participant in AA for a number of years. On moving to Los Angeles she had quickly found a new group and established a new relationship with a sponsor, and she attended meetings regularly. She no longer drank or engaged in other forms of substance abuse, except for smoking cigarettes. Her abstinence continued throughout the analysis.

Two events in her childhood appear to have been decisive for Ms. A.'s psychological development. First, when she was two, her maternal grandmother died. The grandmother had been living with the family, and Ms. A. remembers being close to her. Ms. A. reports that her mother said that after the grandmother's death Ms. A. became much more shy, withdrawn, and self-centered. Ms. A. also recalls her mother as being so deeply disturbed by the loss that she refused to leave the house for nearly a year. Apparently Ms. A.'s mother was deeply depressed by her own mother's death, and this event may have fostered her close identification with her daughter.

The second event, which occurred around Ms. A.'s seventh birthday, enhanced the symbiotic attachment between mother and daughter. Ms. A.'s aunt—her mother's sister, who had been living with the family for several years—died. This aunt had expressed great warmth toward Ms. A., in contrast to the coolness of the rest of the family. Ms. A. felt her loss deeply, so deeply that she refused to tell people outside the family, such as her teacher, about the death. She remembers trying for a time to deny its reality. Her mother again turned to her for solace. Ms. A. vividly remembers her mother's overwhelming sense of loss for her sister. She also remembers her own powerful and confusing feelings when her mother took her to the mortuary to help pick out the casket and asked her for opinions about the details of the funeral arrangements. She wondered why it was she who held this special place for her mother, and not her father or another member of the family.

Also around this time, Ms. A.'s father's alcoholism was more severe and the conflict between her parents was more intense than ever. She remembers wondering whether to buy an anniversary present for her parents because she was not sure the marriage would survive until the anniversary. It was an unfortunate coincidence, given the intensity of the mother-daughter relationship, that Ms. A.'s birthday fell on the same day as her parents' anniversary. As Ms. A. remembers it, her mother would never acknowledge her birthday until Ms. A. first remembered the anniversary. Finally, at about this time, Ms. A.'s oldest brother, about eleven years older than she, eloped with a woman of different ethnic background and religion. This was devastating for Ms. A.'s mother. Here was another family embarrassment, and Ms. A. once again was called upon to share in her mother's disapproval of a family member. All these incidents, which occurred around her seventh birthday, underscored for Ms. A. her mother's special need for her and the unpredictability of the outside world, and so they strengthened her bond with her mother. Throughout Ms. A.'s adolescence, this special connection never weakened. While Ms. A. was eager to go to college and to pursue a career, she also believed that her mother could not tolerate her leaving. In striking out on her own, she struggled with guilt for abandoning her mother and a concern—of which she was less aware—that she could not make her way without her mother's strong presence in her life.

Not surprisingly, Ms. A.'s relationships with men, after she left the family, were fraught with difficulty. Each man came to represent a threat to her symbiotic tie with her mother. Although consciously she thought she had broken with her mother, and had even rebelled against her, the tie was still strong. The result was a history of unsatisfactory relationships.

Her first boyfriend, whom she had been dating for nearly a year, suddenly announced that he was homosexual and left her. During her analysis she stayed in contact with him, consoling him when he learned that he was HIV positive. A second boyfriend suffered from serious depression. While they were involved he committed suicide, and she discovered him dead in his apartment. She kept in touch with his family, remembering with them each anniversary of his death. When she began treatment she announced that she was in a not altogether satisfactory relationship. The relationship had begun as a sexual one, but many months had passed since the couple had had sexual relations. And finally, perhaps her closest confidant was a young man whom she had known for several years and who coincidentally had moved to Los Angeles about the same time she had. Several months after her analysis began he was diagnosed as having AIDS, and he died shortly thereafter.

A good deal of Ms. A.'s time was spent in remembering—memorializing—these various losses. She was ever vigilant that she not ignore the anniversary of any of these deaths. She also marked other anniversaries, such as the beginning of her sobriety.

Our work began with meetings twice a week. Ms. A. was highly motivated to feel better, and I was very taken with her capacity to face her many traumatizing experiences and to consider her own contribution to them. She seemed convinced that this long, difficult road of self-examination would lead to more happiness and contentment than she had thus far experienced. Her confidence that the analysis would yield such positive results seemed surprising, given the hardships and losses of her life.

We soon were meeting four times a week and, toward the end of the analysis, five times a week. For a short time during the crisis period that I will describe we met six times a week.

It became increasingly clear to me that the most important work in the treatment revolved around the analysis of the relationship between the two of us: the transference relationship. Ms. A.'s earliest relationships and other, later ones were very intense. In this she was no different from any of us. What was remarkable was that for her each and every relationship proved to be deeply disappointing. I came to believe that the best way to discover her unconscious contribution to these relationships and to disentangle the past from the present was to explore the ways in which our relationship was being set up to be similarly disappointing. Ms. A.'s commitment to the treatment facilitated this kind of analytic work: determined to make the analysis a success, she embraced, yet again, an intense personal relationship—with me. I felt I had no choice but to respond with a like intensity and work to ensure an outcome different from those she had experienced in the past. If her strong desire for—we might say her insistence on—a meaningful relationship with me was driven, at least in part, by a repetition compulsion, it was my task to see to it that this relationship would not end in disappointment.

Ms. A.'s motivation boded well for a successful analytic outcome, but the process itself was by no means easy for either of us. In many ways Ms. A. was a compliant patient who sought to do what she imagined I expected of her. And yet she tried hard to avoid bringing any powerful feelings to our work. Later in the analysis she became aware that at the outset she had hoped that her problem might be "surgically removed" in a way that did not have to engage her emotions. Her fantasy had been that she might be operated on painlessly, without any loss of blood. She had hoped to develop the necessary intense relationship with me without having any feelings for or about me.

Although she was able, in the first months, to talk about having erotic fantasies, and even about suppressing such fantasies for fear I would interpret them as being about me, she was unable to bring the fantasies directly into the treatment. She also avoided telling me her dreams. On occasion she did present some vivid dream material that I believed expressed the centrality of the therapy in her psychic life, but these were extremely difficult sessions. Revealing these dreams to me made her feel far too vulnerable, both to the feelings she was acknowledging and to the ways I might use the information.

For two or three months Ms. A. expressed great reluctance to use the couch. This was one example of her anxiety about appearing to be like a child and indicated her formidable efforts to maintain an adult, conscious, mature persona. It recapitulated her original complaint: the disjuncture between the way she presented herself and was perceived by others and the way she felt inside.

Ms. A.'s apparent compliance, it became clear, was actually a pseudocompliance, intended to keep her more assertive, "naughty" self out of the analysis. This was the present-day expression of a life-long struggle. Her symbiotic attachment to her mother, her religious piety, and her compliance, on the one side, and her self-abuse through smoking, drinking, and promiscuity, on the other, constituted the dynamic conflict in her life. Its purpose was to suppress the expression of her own personal needs and desires—different from those of her mother—as well as to subdue her anger at those who had failed to protect and nurture her fragile, small self.

Ms. A.'s attraction to self-absorbed, depressed men, perhaps with ambivalent sexual identities, seemed to me to express an unconscious preference for those invulnerable to her anger and rage. Because they effectively disclaimed interest in her, she did not need to fear her own destructive, demanding impulses. In this "solution," she was able to present herself as the compliant, concerned, self-denying person: her angry, demanding, independent, and naughty self could remain secret, hidden from view and detached from her own experience. Furthermore, her masochistic pattern of involvement with people who needed her but provided her with little sustenance was a repetition of her relationship with her mother and also filled the space that would otherwise have been occupied by her own needs and by her anger at those who denied her opportunities for self-expression. But the series of rejections she faced from men and the deaths she experienced, all in a relatively short time, prevented this attempted resolution from working for her.

Her involvement with Alcoholics Anonymous, I believe, enabled her to experience, for the first time, her *self*, however fragile, and provided a context in which she was able to seek therapy. Perhaps, too, the fervency characteristic of such self-help groups helped imbue Ms. A. with her steely determination to ensure, despite all her defenses, that her therapy would work.

In the sixth month of the analysis Ms. A. suddenly learned that her mother was terminally ill and had only weeks to live. She was diagnosed with inoperable cancer and chose to remain at home for the duration of her life. In the following weeks Ms. A. took many brief trips home, witnessing her mother's rapid deterioration. During the last visits her mother, although alert, no longer recognized her. As her mother's condition worsened, Ms. A.'s attention shifted to the different ways in which her father and her siblings were responding to her mother's dying, and to the memories stimulated by family members being back in contact with one another after many years of being apart.

On the surface the analytic work shifted dramatically, but in fact the themes marked out previously continued to inform our sessions. Although the manifest content was now her inconsolable feelings about her mother's impending death, Ms. A. continued to struggle with her efforts to shelter herself, and me, from unacceptable emotions, and I continued to focus on these internal conflicts. Ms. A. worried about the intensity of her feelings, believing that she alone was finding the imminent loss of her mother so unbearable, while other family members must be coping better. She also imagined that I was impatient with her pain and frustrated by her inability to function normally despite her mother's dying. I believe that at this time Ms. A. was experiencing me as something of a mother figure: as someone who, like her mother, could prevent the expression of her intolerable needs and feelings, instead encouraging her to meet my expectations of appropriate behavior.

Around this time there was evidence of the development of the transference neurosis, a point in a psychoanalysis when the analytic relationship becomes the most important feature of the patient's life and the feelings concerning the treatment make all other life experiences pale in comparison. The analysis fills the foreground for the patient; "life itself" is, for a time, in the background. Despite her mother's condition, Ms. A. became preoccupied with a comment of mine—one that had no direct bearing on her mother's illness or impending death—that she experienced as wrong. In response to a dream that she described, I commented that she wanted to be the center of attention; she wanted to be the most important person around. Her immediate reaction was to accept my statement and to remain compliant, but after the session she felt enraged by my insensitivity. Despite extensive work in subsequent sessions, her rage did not dissipate, and she could not rid herself of powerful impulses to stop treatment. In the fifth session where this was discussed, she acknowledged that her intense reaction did not fit my "crime," and she said that her anger toward me was probably a deflection of the rage she felt toward her mother for abandoning her. Her mother's illness required that she repress her long-held hostile feelings (now surfacing partly as a result of her relationship with me) and prevented her from experiencing her angry feelings about her mother's imminent death.

Ms. A.'s mother died, and she was extremely sad. She was now able to experience more vividly her strong bond with her mother and to recognize the way that bond had protected her from her anxiety about autonomy. For a time she was able to acknowledge, albeit tentatively, a sense of being liberated from her mother's control, a feeling of freedom that she found both confusing and exhilarating. Later sessions would reveal that Ms. A. unconsciously experienced her mother's death as a personal victory, and in the subsequent months she vacillated between feelings of extraordinary liberation and feelings of intense anxiety that she was alone and unprotected from her own sexuality and her desires for recognition and achievement.

During the analysis the tug of war between these conflicting feelings intensified. On the one side, Ms. A. became determined to deny her sexuality, attempting to experience men, including me, as benign protectors who would contain her sexual interests rather than exploit them. On the other side, her mother's death propelled her toward a greater acceptance of her own body and feelings, as for the first time she felt free to experience herself as separate from her mother. She paid more attention to her physical appearance: she lost weight, allowed her fingernails to grow and polished them, and purchased new, more fashionable clothes. This exploration of her femininity had begun prior to her mother's death and continued after her mother died.

Ms. A. was also reporting a renewal of her relationship with her father. She could appreciate him for the first time, being able to view him through lenses different from the harsh, demeaning, critical ones imposed on her by her mother and, until now, internalized as her own. She said it would be ironic if her mother's death enabled her to develop a warm and loving relationship with her father. While Ms. A. welcomed this kind of liberation, she did not realize that what would be liberated was sexual longings and desires for recognition. These were needs, she was to learn, that no one—not her father, her boyfriend, her other friends, or her analyst—could contain.

Childhood Sexual Abuse Remembered

Three months after her mother died Ms. A. found herself in a personal crisis. She was experiencing intense anger at friends and relatives who she believed had failed or betrayed her, and was feeling extraordinarily alone in her suffering. She was hoping, in her analysis, to re-create the time when, early in her life, she had felt secure and protected by her father. She had already produced memories of this period and recalled a pivotal experience—a screen memory—in which she, for the first time, saw her father not as a protector but, like her older brothers, as a sexual predator. This was a memory of the family sitting together watching a movie on television when Ms. A. was probably ten or eleven years old. On the screen, a sexually charged scene between a man and a woman was being portrayed. Ms. A. remembers her mother and sisters recoiling from the scene, pulling back and averting their eyes. Her father and brothers, however, pulled themselves closer to the screen, intently interested in the sex and clearly enjoying it. She discovered that men had impulses other than protective ones toward girls and women, a discovery that made her feel terribly vulnerable.

She now wanted the analytic relationship to compensate for the loneliness and isolation she was feeling. In one session, for example, she imagined sitting on my lap rather than using the couch. The fantasy frightened her; she feared that what began as a childish wish might become a sexual encounter. She could not experience the wish to be safe with me without the intrusion of dangerous sexual feelings, ones that she feared might overwhelm both of us. Even though I commented on this conflict as it developed, the intensity of the feelings and her strategies to defend against them threatened, at various times, to disrupt the analytic process.

In one session, after several in which Ms. A. described her positive feelings about her analysis and how safe she felt during the analytic hour, she reported the following dream:

> This was a dream of a woman who was trying to kill me, but no matter what she did, I knew she couldn't kill me. This woman was doing strange, weird things, almost demonic, wanting to kill and trying to figure all these ways to kill. But I knew that the knife would not let her kill me. There was something I did to the knife that won't let her kill me. It was scary, but I didn't feel the terror . . . I think it's a fairly significant dream, and I think of the word blessed, but I don't know what I did to the knife.

I compared this dream, which we came to call the "blessed knife" dream, to another dream, reported earlier, that also featured a woman intent on killing her. In that dream, Ms. A. was terrified and had to escape. I noted that the safety she felt in the new dream was quite different from her feeling in the earlier one. She readily agreed, and said, "I left here yesterday thinking that I like how I feel, and I want to feel that way, and whatever I need to do to keep my self, I'll do it."

"To bless the knife," I offered.

"If I have to come here totally anxious, then that's the price I'll pay to feel that way. It's like I made a pact with myself, just acknowledging that I like feeling good."

I responded, "Though there are apparently strong forces within you that are trying to prevent this."

She agreed and said she no longer felt terrorized by those feelings and remarked on how new an experience that was for her. I was struck by her inadvertent admission that she often felt "totally anxious" about coming to her analytic sessions. I silently wondered whether she thought she could reduce her anxiety by trying to "bless me." Perhaps a key aim was to disarm me sexually so that I could not interfere with the feeling of safety that she enjoyed with me, and that gave her such a positive feeling about herself.

In the next several sessions Ms. A. complained of feeling "off-center," of having "tension knots" in her stomach, of being unable to feel free of anxiety. I returned to the blessed knife dream and suggested that it expressed a wish to do away with her own sexual and other inappropriate feelings. Her anxiety expressed an inability to get rid of those feelings, which bubbled beneath the surface and could not be contained. She responded by remembering a dream she had had three days earlier but, until that moment, had forgotten:

> I was in this outside area, where there were thatched open huts. There were beds in each of the huts. I had to

go to the bathroom; I was with somebody but I went into this hut, and there was this guy. Somehow I was supposed to look at the different beds—it was sexual—and I was supposed to have sex with one of these people in the beds. I opened up the covers of one, and it was a baby, a little baby girl. I said, but it's a baby, and I started sobbing. The baby was lifeless and had been abused so much, and she had a tumor in her stomach. I couldn't look at her face anymore, and I started sobbing.

I woke up. I can remember the look on her face, she was probably about two. This look, like she wasn't alive, and she had just been so—like a thing. It was upsetting. Was it upsetting because I had sexual feelings for her, or because it was kind of horrible—it's a baby! She looked so sad, and then I thought it was part of me, I'm afraid it was something I'd repressed, or didn't remember, but it's like I could know how she felt by just looking at her—a strange feeling, it was like "I don't care what you do to me, there's a place that's my own, and I'm not really here."

After reporting the dream, Ms. A. discussed it: "It was like she (the baby) just said, 'I'm just not going to be here. I'm not going to be here, you can do to me what you want. I'm just going to check out.'"

"Take leave," I said.

"Yes, but then I don't feel happy, split off. But I did feel that was a part of her that was there, that was protected. They just got her body, but she held on to who she was, and that's what I've felt when I've been happy, that part of me has been able to come out."

I asked her to talk about the sexual feelings in the dream.

"I don't know if that's why I didn't talk about it during

the week. It was so strange. I was supposed—there were people there to be used and I was supposed to have sex; the guy—the one showing me the beds—was real cute, and I was having sexual feelings about him, and then I saw this baby and I was appalled. I just remember this little girl—part of the horror was my own sexual feelings. I don't know if they were for her, and then I was ashamed that I had any sexual feelings at all."

I suggested that the dream expressed a need, one she had felt at the age of two, to merge with the baby—the injured and lifeless girl—that her mother wanted her to be. (I was remembering the mother's report of Ms. A.'s state of mind following the death of her grandmother.) The need to merge was a way to ward off the sexual, life-affirming feelings that she had about the cute guy. What came to my mind as I heard her associations, in short, was pre-oedipal material, based upon Ms. A.'s early history. In retrospect, I might also have focused more clearly on her current relationship with me. I could have suggested that the feelings of sexuality were so frightening that the dream expressed her (futile) wish to split off, in the analysis, her sexual feelings—her body—from her soul or spirit. But it seemed to me that the dream crystallized the conflict she had been experiencing since the death of her mother, and revealed her increasing difficulty in keeping sexual, self-assertive feelings from overwhelming her sense of being safe and protected.

Through this dream analysis, I felt we had made substantial headway toward disentangling this central psychic conflict. I expected the next sessions to focus on her feelings about sexuality, and on what terrified her about it. But I miscalculated. As I now see it, Ms. A. chose an alternative "solution" to the conflict: instead of exploring the strength of her autonomous striving—her thwarted attraction to the "cute guy"—she used the dream as evidence that all her life she had been confronted with real dangers.

In the next session Ms. A. was extremely agitated and angry with me. She insisted that my interpretation of the dream was mistaken and my intervention a distraction. She believed the dream was about her own sexual abuse by her father when she was very young. She confessed, for the first time, to long-standing suspicions that she had been abused; and she hypothesized that because of the positive relationship that she had established with me, she was now able to recover some of the feelings about it, if not actual memories.

In the following days Ms. A. experienced severe panic reactions. One evening, for example, she felt compelled to retreat into her bathtub; she speculated that in her childhood the bathroom had been the only room that could be locked and, therefore, the only room where she could feel safe. Only by making plans to sleep at a friend's house did Ms. A. feel safe enough to leave the bathtub. On succeeding nights she began writing letters to the little girl in the dream in an effort to uncover the truth of what had happened between her and her father.

Ms. A. was finding it more and more difficult to conduct her life normally. Her work suffered; she had increasing trouble concentrating in class or focusing on her research and writing. She began to read voraciously about "adult survivors" of childhood incest, and she asked me for permission to attend a meeting of these survivors. Concerned that I was not sufficiently attuned to the problems of incest victims, she recommended books and articles for me to read. She also requested an additional weekly analytic session, and we began to see each other six times a week.

Because her father sometimes babysat for his young granddaughters, Ms. A. felt obliged both to accuse her father of incest and to tell all her siblings about it. To her surprise, her father, although stung by the charges and having no recollection of abuse, nonetheless conceded that since he had experienced alcoholic blackouts, such abuse might have occurred when he was drunk. "If my daughter, whom I love dearly, remembers it," he said, "then it might have happened." "And," he added, "Satan works in strange and unpredictable ways." In response to her accusations, some of her siblings were defensive of their father and hostile to her; others were more sympathetic to her. For her part, Ms. A. decided to break off communication with her father and with most of her siblings.

Ms. A.'s case demonstrates how difficult negotiating the past in the context of the present can be. Our work together had been characterized by her impressive capacity to present vivid and compelling fragments of experience from quite early in her childhood. Deeply disturbing moments from quite an early age—for example, the deaths of her grandmother and her aunt—were recalled through descriptions of specific incidents that were powerfully and lucidly lodged in her memory. For example, she described an early memory of a roomful of adults in her house after her grandmother died, and her account of her trip to the mortuary when her aunt died was a vivid vignette documenting the power of her aunt's death in her young life. When she offered a "new" memory, it was typically linked to some associative logic that I was able to recognize. Discussing feelings of being abandoned might yield a new memory of a childhood experience of being left alone, or of feeling unprotected. For example, her memories of watching a movie on television with her family and of being left alone with her older brothers and sisters were associated with current emotional states. There was a kind of chain-link connection between one experience and some subsequent recollection.

As a result of Ms. A.'s ability to provide vivid descriptions of important moments in her life, I viewed her as having a "good" memory, and a representational one. I found myself relatively unconcerned about what in my work with other patients I consider my responsibility to encourage and promote the recollection of early experiences. The task of recovering her early history I increasingly entrusted to Ms. A., confident of her ability to do so without my intervention. Indeed, her production of a memory of abuse might well have sprung from the analytic world we constructed together—had it been achieved in the same way as her production of other memories.

But these particular memories of early sexual abuse seemed to me to be of a different character. She was describing dramatically revelatory experiences that seemed to me unconnected to contemporary affective themes in our work together. Ms. A. was distraught when describing herself as a victim of sexual abuse, but no specific vignettes comparable to her other early memories accompanied this distress. She concluded that the incest had occurred when she was very young—two years old or so—because she did not have vivid recollections but only the suspicion of its occurrence. Her most vivid memory was one she did not describe until after she had changed her mind about the incest: she recalled her father leaning over her bed in his boxer shorts, with his genitals visible through the underwear's fly; she also remembered her mother yelling at him for this indiscretion. This memory, which had the qualities of other early memories such as the one of her trip to the mortuary with her mother, she shared with me much later in the analysis as evidence of her father's probable innocence. But when she first accused her father, what she was remembering was her childhood feelings of being unprotected and vulnerable. She concluded at the time that only childhood incest could explain such powerful and unhappy emotional experiences. Of course, the lack of vividness might have derived from the troubling nature of the memories and from Ms. A.'s efforts to keep them from surfacing. But because of the disparity between the vivid memories that corresponded to certain dominant themes in her analysis and these vague memories of incest, I experienced the latter as inauthentic.

I was not confident, however, in my own skeptical reactions. My distrust derived largely from the popular psychology that enveloped our analytic relationship—the folk wisdom of the moment. The recovery of long-repressed experiences of childhood sexual abuse and the acknowledgment of how much more widespread such abuse was than had previously been known were at the time the stuff of both professional and public parlance. We were living in an age intolerant of past efforts to sweep these shocking experiences under the rug. In this atmosphere, I was not sure whether my discomfort with Ms. A.'s memories arose from the perturbation I sensed in the relationship we had established together or from the disturbing character of the memories themselves. It was difficult, in this context, to keep the analytic relationship in the foreground, the surrounding environment in the background.

Nonetheless, I continued—with the support of my supervisor—to consider the possibility that I was witnessing an analytic enactment in which Ms. A. was unconsciously exploiting the interpersonal roles that we had by now comfortably settled into: she the storyteller, recounting her past, I the trusting and appreciative listener. My skepticism, too, could be understood as a product of the idiosyncratic relationship we had constructed together. I experienced her as abusing her storyteller's role. With these new kinds of memories she was changing both the nature of the story and its narrative form. She presented me now with a story about trauma and abuse—about real villains inflicting harm on her—rather than one about unbearable psychic suffering. And this story, in contrast to earlier ones, was not told in specific and detailed vignettes of painful encounters within herself and with others. Now she offered only an evocative tale of victimization, far less distinct than I had come to expect from her. In my skepticism I resisted her effort to change the terms of our relationship.

The production of these memories also altered our relationship in other ways. First, Ms. A. became less and less capable of differentiating the past from the present: she experienced the remembered trauma as if she were currently its victim. In the memories of childhood sexual abuse, Ms. A. was no longer differentiating between herself as the experiencer and the experience itself. The present merged with the past; her memories of the abuse fused with the conduct of her current life. The memory of abuse served, in a perverse way, both as solace and as license to alter her relations with family, friends, and other intimates, including me. She regressed to acting as she imagined the child that had been injured had acted, as if the abuse were occurring in the present. She feared being alone. She retreated to the safety of her locked bathroom. She lost her capacity to be responsible as an adult in her work and in her relationships with others. For a time, she became the injured child she was now remembering as having been abused in the past.

Second, the boundaries that had been established between us, clearly demarcating the separateness of our selves, came under powerful attack. The pressure on me to corroborate these memories was unusually strong; for Ms. A., the reality of her past abuse depended, in some significant sense, upon my affirmation of it. My collaboration with her recollections became as important as the memories themselves. She wished, I believe, to identify with me, to achieve an undifferentiated link between her memories and my sympathy. Hans Loewald describes these as identificatory memories. In contrast to memories that represent the past, these express a fusion with the remembered past. They are memories experienced not representationally but as unmediated, unconsciously experienced bodily states.[2]

Although these features—the difficulty in distinguishing past from present and the blurring of boundaries—may characterize some analytic relationships, until then they had not been characteristic of *our* relationship, even at times when Ms. A. was exploring a more regressed or childlike state of being. These new dimensions did not seem to be part of the developmental continuum that one comes to expect in a deepening analytic relationship, but rather seemed to me to represent her unconscious effort to destroy the relationship itself.

I was deeply troubled by the pain Ms. A. was experiencing and by the intrusion of her past into her current suffering. But the specific ways in which she now diverged from our previously established styles of communicating helped me resist the impulse to overcome my own deeply personal reaction to her remembering and to comply with her demands. What was striking was that her emotional state allowed for no "space in between," no room for joint reflection, for mediation, or for complexity. Her memories seemed to me to be an attack on the very ground of our mutual, intersubjectively constituted existence, an effort to destroy the arena that we had built for ourselves to work in. My challenge was to maintain the precarious, hard-won relationship we had constructed together over the past year and one-half, in spite of Ms. A.'s efforts to return to a more familiar, albeit unsatisfying, pattern of relating to others by either rejecting them or symbiotically identifying with them. I had to resist my own predilection to respond sympathetically and supportively by simply affirming her memories.

Through our intense work together we had developed our own expectations of each other, profound feelings, beliefs, and fantasies. They constituted the intersubjective field through which our analytic work was conducted. Ms. A., I now realize, attempted for a time to destroy that field and to eliminate the possibility that the analysis might become a genuinely transformative experience—for her, but for me as well. And my ability to *know* our relationship, to accept its particular character, and to trust what I knew about it, allowed me to maintain my independence (though I don't want to underemphasize the counterpressures I was experiencing).

But somehow—for many reasons, including my analytic training, the guidance of my supervisor, and Ms. A.'s strength in not insisting too hard that I capitulate to her demands—I managed to preserve my capacity for independent reason, judgment, and evaluation. As a result, we were able to chart a new and different path in our relationship. It provided the foundation upon which Ms. A. could establish both a new relation to her past and a new pattern of relating to others in the present that marked the success of our analytic work together.

I present this case, then, not only to recount what I believe to be its successful outcome. More important, it is a cautionary tale against, first, a premature certainty about childhood trauma's impact on present-day psychology, and, second, premature capitulation on the analyst's part to what may be transitory subjective experiences of the patient. Ms. A.'s thinking and behavior were attempts, I believe, to preserve her own alienation. By attacking me, her father, and the analysis, she was unwittingly marshalling all the resources at her command to ensure her own social and personal isolation.

There is, of course, no telling what might have happened had I capitulated to Ms. A.'s demands that I corroborate her story about childhood sexual abuse. Nor is there any certainty that Ms. A.'s eventual conclusions about the role of fantasy in her feelings toward her father were not influenced by my skepticism. But it does seem clear that Ms. A.'s belief that she had been sexually abused derived as much from her present-day psychic conflicts and difficulty in establishing new patterns of interpersonal relating as from *anything* that may have happened to her in childhood.

Thus far I have described the crisis in Ms. A.'s analysis from a psychodynamic perspective. But the broader sociocultural context surely played a role as well. This broader context will be the subject of subsequent chapters, but it is important to acknowledge here the peculiar intersection of Ms. A.'s memories and my ambivalent response to them with the cultural discourses affecting us. We were both, I believe, having trouble differentiating our particular experience with each other from the social context in which our encounter was happening.

At this time, for example, I was feeling vulnerable to the cultural critique that had been leveled not only at analysts but at men in general as being unwilling to enter women's "psychic reality" and to appreciate the degree of oppression and subordination of women in this patriarchal society. In many respects I had distanced myself from these charges, believing that, for various reasons, I was not guilty of such prejudice. But I came to realize that my personal convictions had never faced a direct challenge from another person. Ms. A. was now making me feel very much the unresponsive male—stern, withholding, and without understanding of female experience. My "analytic stance" seemed more and more like a defensive posture in which I was withdrawing from genuine involvement with my patient's pain so as to protect myself. I couldn't help wondering whether I was also defending the status quo, denying women's reality and affirming a logico-rational, male order of which I had long been a beneficiary. Had sexual politics—hers and mine—overwhelmed psychoanalysis?

In retrospect it seems quite clear that Ms. A. was also strongly affected, though largely unconsciously, by the stories of childhood abuse and repressed memory that were so prominent at the time. And it is striking how little I participated in the discourse about these issues; I missed what I now see were obvious references to it. If Ms. A. was overwhelmed by the cultural moment, as I came to believe, I was underinvolved in it.

Our different reactions to the narratives of trauma and abuse that were so salient in the cultural landscape contributed to the misunderstandings that were part of our analytic relationship at the time. Consider, for example, Ms. A.'s reporting of the dream about the abused baby. She concluded by saying, "and then I thought it [the baby] was part of me, *I'm afraid it was something I'd repressed, or didn't remember . . .*" For all intents and purposes, Ms. A. was announcing that she believed she was one of the many who had been sexually abused in childhood. Had I understood the social references when they were first reported, I might have responded differently, even while remaining reluctant to embrace her narrative fully. But, unaware of the cultural context, I focused on other dimensions of the dream, not recognizing the narrative frame that Ms. A. was apparently adopting and thus failing to understand the unconscious or implicit concerns that her interpretation implied, concerns that may even have generated the dream in the first place.

In the days after she reported this dream, Ms. A., you may recall, began writing to "the child within," the part of her where the actual memories of abuse were stored, which had remained inaccessible to her for years. Through this technique she hoped to recover the "truth" of what had happened to her when she was very young. The idea of an "inner child" was a psychological construct developed largely by participants in the "recovered memory movement." Ms. A. wanted me to read Ellen Bass and Laura Davis's book *The Courage to Heal: A Guide for Women Survivors of Child Sexual Abuse*. This was far and away the most popular contemporary guidebook for "survivors" of sexual abuse, having sold more than 750,000 copies in its first two editions. Bass and Davis recommend that their readers try writing to "the child within": "If you're capable of loving and comforting the child within, if you can let your adult self express the compassion you have for this child, write to her now and let her know."[3]

Ms. A.'s central dream had a striking resemblance to a vignette in their book. In a chapter on grieving and mourning one's past, Bass and Davis include a statement made by one of their clients:

I went down to see the children inside me. The first one I noticed just sat on the curb in my abdomen. She'd sit there with her head in her hand, looking very sad, or she'd be jumping up and down, being manic. Then there was one in my heart who would sit in a room behind a door. She'd open the door and peek out, and then shut the door, 'cause she got scared. Then there was the one who was dead . . . I sobbed and mourned that a part of me had died.[4]

This paragraph dramatically parallels Ms. A.'s own dream

of seeing row after row of babies, one of whom she discovered had been abused. I do not know whether Ms. A. read this book before or after she had the dream, but it seems certain that the book influenced her view of herself as a "survivor."

In this regard, the rupture that we experienced in our relationship was a culturally induced one: Ms. A. embraced the language, imagery, and affect of the recovered memory movement while I was so untouched by this movement that I was unable to recognize its impact on her. Perhaps I should have been more responsive to her insistence that I read books about childhood abuse and its aftermath. But my resistance expressed my concern that if I immersed myself in this literature I might lose the ability to differentiate between the individual reality of my patient and the cultural reality of a social movement intent on exposing problems in the society—the physical and sexual abuse of children—that had for too long been hidden. This concern was especially pertinent, I believe, because a prominent feature of the discourse around recovered memory was an insistence on bifurcating the world into friends and enemies, victims and perpetrators. Either one embraced the imagery, or one was part of the problem. Thus, at the time, the opportunity for a disinterested exploration or for open inquiry was severely constricted. In this way the cultural phenomenon evinced the same kind of constriction that was occurring in the analytic setting itself. I worried that if I learned more about childhood abuse and recovered memory my sociology would come to the fore, making it more difficult for me to keep Ms. A.'s individual life and her relationships with myself and others at the center of our work together.

As weeks and months passed without Ms. A.'s conveying any specific or elaborated images of abuse, I became increasingly convinced that she had come to believe in the abuse as a way of defending against the intensity of her positive and sexualized feelings for me. In effect, Ms. A. was attempting to keep her soul in analysis while leaving her body—her sexuality, self-needs, and strivings for autonomy—out of it. She was trying to give her injured body over to the father of her childhood. She was also reexperiencing her own powerful and positive feelings toward her father, feelings set free by our work together and by the release she felt after her mother's death. Yet she sought to convert her sexualized desire into his crime. With me, she hoped to control her eroticized feelings by having me collude with her historical reconstruction. Had she succeeded in this endeavor, her gain would have been substantial and well worth the pain that she endured in the process. She would have been able to sacrifice the father of her childhood, disavow her sexuality and autonomous strivings, and preserve the safe and secure relationship with me that had existed before she discovered the dangers of her sexuality.

Over time my own conviction became stronger—though never certain—that, despite her insistence, she had not been sexually abused. I did not challenge her version of things and attempted to maintain a kind of analytic neutrality. But, because I did not corroborate her presentation, she sensed my reluctance to believe her version of events. I felt strong pressure to provide solace through what I came to think would have been a form of collusion. Had I shared in her version of things, we would together have concluded that the intense inner conflicts she was experiencing in her current relationships—with me, with her father, with other men—were to be explained by sexual abuse in early childhood. She was seeking, I believe, the comfort of viewing herself as an innocent victim of horrible abuse, and she was demanding that I agree with her.

It might have been possible both to affirm those memories and eventually to move beyond them. But at the time I felt I had to choose between two diametrically opposed positions: I could either corroborate her memories of abuse and take my place as the symbiotic twin to herself as victim, or I could resist that pattern's repetition and provide a new way of relating that allowed for the growth of her own autonomy. In other words, Ms. A. wanted to keep me as an all-protective paternal figure, one who, in condemning with her her father's sexuality, would enable her to preserve a view of herself as the innocent victim of sexual impulses, not as a possessor of them. She sought to cloak herself in victimization, thereby renouncing responsibility for her own self-needs or sexual longings. I felt it was important to resist that inclination.

The Way Back

Over time the analysis became less volatile and the crisis surrounding childhood abuse receded. Ms. A. discussed abuse less and less often, only occasionally remarking that she felt I did not believe her version of events. In some dream material she revealed her own skepticism that her father had abused her, but she still communicated with him only infrequently. She seemed reluctant to express her own doubts about the reality of the abuse, apparently fearing that I would affirm those doubts. This reluctance sprang from an important shift in our relationship that occurred a result of the crisis: Ms. A. came to experience me less as the early childhood paternal figure who she hoped would protect her, and more as the all-enveloping, sometimes frustrating maternal figure without whom she feared she was unable to live. The childish wish to remain ever passive, secure in the father's protection, gave way to a feeling of being joined together with a mother-analyst who sometimes did not appreciate how necessary she was to her daughter's survival.

To illustrate this shift in our relationship, recall that during the crisis Ms. A. requested a sixth weekly appointment with me, and we agreed to meet on Saturdays until the crisis abated. It has been suggested to me that I was wrong to change the frame of the psychoanalysis in this way and that doing so intensified Ms. A.'s confusion. To be sure, my willingness to see Ms. A. a sixth time, while largely a response to her pain, also derived from my own feeling of guilt—or let us call it my ambivalence—about not accepting her rendering of the past. I believed that my unresponsiveness was adding to her suffering and I sought to make up for that through a sixth session.

After several Saturday appointments, and when it was clear that Ms. A. was functioning more cohesively, I told her that I would no longer see her on Saturdays. Although she agreed that she no longer needed the extra appointments, she was deeply wounded by my unilateral decision and, more important, she was disappointed that she would no longer have this "special" Saturday appointment with me. This was a reaction, however, that she became aware of only gradually. On the Monday after the first Saturday on which we did not meet, she reported the following dream:

It was during the session. Mr. D. [a fellow student whom she had previously described as someone she felt she could not confide in during her crisis and who, at times, reminded her of her father] was there, sitting in a chair. I was talking about something, and it was really vivid, and I slid off the couch and had a temper tantrum, kicking my legs. I didn't want him there but it felt kind of good to have a temper tantrum.

Then you picked me up and put me around the doorway—I kind of bent around to fit through the door—and I finally pulled myself together and I was going to go home, but you invited me to your home. When I saw the house, I said, "I know the house," and I met your kids—you had an older kid—lots of kids, and I met your wife—blonde, pretty—and I had dinner.

And then we were in a group, and you had a different woman on your lap who wasn't your wife, and I didn't know who she was. And she was talking about something important to you about the group, and you started rubbing her breasts. I was surprised—why is he doing this?—and I was sad that I was going to have to leave. And I thought, "Now I know where he lives, in relation to my parents' home. I can drive by."

After she described the dream she was unable to associate freely to it, except to say that it was extremely vivid. She had not wanted to report it to me, though she could not stop thinking about it. My own thought—my working hypothesis—was that the events in the dream expressed her feelings about our special meetings, meetings that (she imagined) took me away from my family on weekends. As I heard the dream, I thought that the temper tantrum involving Mr. D. encapsulated the crisis she had created concerning sexual abuse and her father. The result of the crisis was to establish a closer involvement with me, including the change to meeting six times a week. In the dream, she was longing for me to stroke her breasts, a wish that I interpreted as an early childhood—that is, pregenital—desire for closeness and intimacy. But she was aware that she was no longer able to have such intimacy. I asked her how it had felt not to see me the previous Saturday. Ms. A. simply said that she had not missed the Saturday appointment as much as she had expected, and then she began talking about the reasons why she could not trust Mr. D.

But in the next session Ms. A. came in enraged with me. She wanted to kill me, she said, because of the humiliation of my cancelling the Saturday appointments. She charged that by not waiting for her to suggest ending them, I was accusing her—accurately, she added—of enjoying the specialness of the Saturday appointments, even after she no longer needed them. By the next session she was no longer angry but instead felt ashamed, "like being caught," she said.

"I liked coming in on Saturdays, and you knew it, and you caught me, and I still feel ashamed."

I said, "You feel ashamed at feeling special."

"It's hard for me to look at," she responded, "but there was something about feeling special, and I didn't even know it." She went on to describe how painful it felt that

I seemed to be so close, that I knew so much about her, and she said that her emotions felt sinful.

"The feeling that you wanted to see me on Saturday, does that feel like a sin?" I asked.

"Yeah, the feelings behind it, the wanting, the feeling special, they are sinful, they really are, you're not supposed to want to feel special. I know it sounds bizarre, but it's true."

Over time Ms. A. developed a capacity to analyze these experiences. She became aware of the powerful role that splitting played in her psychic experience. She came to understand the way her feelings toward me resembled those toward her mother, and now less concerned with how her mother had used their relationship to constrict Ms. A.'s autonomy, she focused on her own efforts to use our relationship to keep her own sexuality and self-needs at bay.

As these understandings developed so, too, did her interest in focusing exclusively on the analysis and on the analytic relationship. Her participation in Alcoholics Anonymous, for example, began to taper off and, by the end of the analysis, had ended entirely. She no longer worried that her desire to remain sober required periodic monitoring by members of the AA community. She was confident that her psychoanalysis could achieve the same effect. Other mechanisms she had used to defuse the analytic experience were replaced by a capacity to interpret their significance. She even stopped observing the anniversary of every death or trauma in her life, as she began to trust her ability to live in the present without having to defuse its dangers by ensuring the intrusion of the past.

These developments in her analysis enabled Ms. A. to begin a rapprochement with her father. At first she understood this as simply putting the past behind her. But by the end of the analysis she had come to realize that her short-lived belief in sexual abuse had been her way of defending against oedipal feelings (her words, not mine), emotions that terrified her both because they made her vulnerable to her father and because they threatened her relationship with her mother. Several months before the end of the analysis, Ms. A. said, "I think the whole thing with the incest with my father was really about feelings now that I couldn't accept—I remember how much I had hated him and I feel the worst thing was the feeling that I couldn't have a mother *and* a father." As Ms. A. understood it, the resumption of a healthy relationship with her father after her mother's death jeopardized her relationship with her mother. To preserve the symbiotic tie with her mother, she felt she had to abjure her strong, positive, and uncritical attraction to her father.

Perhaps the most important result of this work was that Ms. A. was able, for the first time, to develop a healthy sexual relationship with a man her own age. During the termination phase of the analysis, this relationship developed into a very strong connection, and she was able both to hold loving feelings toward him and to accept his loving feelings toward her. The closing phase of the analysis was characterized by a consolidation of these psychic gains and significant experimentation with a strengthened sense of her own autonomy. She gained great insight into how difficult it was for her to express herself sexually toward her boyfriend without feeling that she was betraying me, her mother-analyst. But with substantial work Ms. A. was able to reconcile strongly dependent feelings toward me with sexual interest in other men. By the end of the analysis, despite some trepidation, she was excited about the possibility of a life independent of me and with her boyfriend.

Two days before the end of the analysis, she presented a final dream: "I was ironing my wedding dress . . . I knew I was going to wear it that day or the next day. I was doing a good job." The dream was about her completion of the analysis and about her capacity, for the first time in her life, to be enthusiastically on her own and in her own world. She told me that she had wanted to get me a gift to mark the end of the analysis, but that nothing could capture how important the analysis had been. I replied that her last dream was her gift to me and to our work together.

Memory in Formation

I have described the case of Ms. A. in some detail to promote the development of a more clinically based understanding of psychological processes. An in-depth case study, focusing on the individual in interpersonal and social context, is useful as we attempt to comprehend the variability of memory: in Ms. A.'s case, how recollections of childhood sexual abuse might be produced at one moment only to give way at another moment to a conviction that no such abuse had occurred. My purpose is not merely to document how fantasies of abuse can be generated by psychic forces that distort early childhood experience—not merely to demonstrate the central psychoanalytic axiom that memories are, as Freud argues, screens that express perceptions of the past generated by interests that postdate the past experiences. That topic is of considerable interest, and I will briefly consider its relevance to Ms. A. But it is not the central theme of this book.

Rather, Ms. A.'s case impels us to consider the ways in which analyst and patient share in the process of memory recovery, reconstructing a history that they jointly experience as an authentically felt narrative linking the patient's past experiences with present-day feelings, ideas, and beliefs. The patient's memory recovery becomes the vehicle for collaboration, the means by which a unique interpersonal and intersubjective field is created in the psychoanalytic setting. The intersubjective relationship is always *in formation* through the recovery of memories; yet while memory consolidates and affirms the connection, it also may serve, as in this case, to derail or destroy it. The central point that I hope to establish is this inextricable connection between contemporary experience and memories of the past.

In Ms. A.'s case, memories of abuse were generated as a result of the experience of analytic intimacy. But it is no less important to acknowledge that the later recognition that Ms. A. had probably *not* been abused was also made possible by the strength of the analytic relationship. This clinical focus on intersubjectivity—what might be described as both the conscious and the unconscious communication that occurs in the dyadic relationship— emphasizes the unique configuration of any analytic relationship. This configuration privileges neither analyst nor patient in the psychodynamic process of psychoanalysis, and generates a particular set of understandings about the relation of an individual's past to his or her present and about the relation between his or her fantasies and reality.[5]

This view of memory as intersubjectively constituted is

an alternative to the polarized positions that currently dominate public discourse about childhood trauma. It also provides a different way to evaluate questions about real or imagined abuse and repressed or recovered memory. If we focus on the process by which history is recovered through remembering and consolidated intersubjectively as real, we will no longer conceptualize memory through exclusive reference to, say, Ms. A.'s psychology or even her past experiences. Rather, we will see that memory is jointly produced between a self and a world of others through which that self is constituted. Ms. A.'s memory recovery was a function of the dyadic psychoanalytic relationship and her current relationships with others. Specifically, our relationship enabled Ms. A., over time, to distinguish between memories of the past that served her contemporary defensive needs and memories that authentically linked past experience with current feelings.

This attention to the dyadic nature of the psychoanalytic process also underscores my premise that memory is not an isolated activity but always a contextual one. The clinical material from Ms. A.'s case is intended to demonstrate that remembering cannot be set apart from the personal, spatial, and temporal context in which it occurs. The case study also sets the stage for a more systematic investigation of the philosophical underpinnings of intersubjectivity (see Chapter 3).

Morton Reiser, a psychoanalyst long interested in the relation between the mind and the brain, has written about the relation between analyst and patient in this process of memory recovery. In *Memory in Mind and Brain* he uses contemporary neuroscientific theory to develop a "relational" theory of brain development, and he identifies the analytic *relationship* as the critical transmuting dimension of psychoanalytic work. Reiser describes the process by which the analyst, receiving over time the patient's memory productions, becomes the patient's "primary recording instrument." The analyst's mental apparatus, Reiser asserts, "selectively detects, records, remembers or forgets, evaluates and reports" what the patient produces over the course of the analysis.[6]

The analyst gradually becomes the receptacle of the patient's memory, making it available for the patient to call up, to associate to, and to comment on in relation to the discourse in the analytic sessions. At least for a time, the analyst is better positioned "to be the patient's memory" than the patient is: because the memories are not the analyst's own, he or she has fewer affective and defensive blocks that might prevent either recall or association. In Reiser's words: "As the work progresses and the patient tells more of the history, more of it is encoded in the analyst's memory, and the overlap or shared portion increases . . . In this way, the analyst, by following the flow of the patient's thoughts, can respond with references to relevant historical material, appropriately phrased. Such communication between the two memory systems clinically manifested as empathy would be mediated or facilitated by overlapping affective tone."[7]

As Reiser makes clear, this kind of memory network constitutes an elaborate and subtle form of psychological communication, though his language of memory systems implies more discrete memory, isolated in the individual, than an intersubjective appreciation of the interpenetrability of memory suggests. Nonetheless, Reiser rightly insists that the memories generated by the patient in concert with the analyst are synonymous with the potentially transformative experience of the analytic encounter: externalizing the patient's mind by having it held by the analyst enables both participants to see it more clearly and allows for the shared discovery of unconscious or preconscious meanings, understandings, and fantasies—encoded as memory—that have constricted and made painful the patient's adult experiences.

The intensity of the analytic relationship and the feeling that she was betraying the memory of her mother were Ms. A.'s most immediate unconscious concerns that threatened to prevent a mutually satisfying analytic experience. They were interfering with her ability to "use" me to develop her human capacities fully. But more impersonal factors were also contributing to Ms. A.'s difficulties in protecting our relationship and in living in the present. Here, sociology helps us understand why her remembering took the form of a memory of incest, elaborated through a narrative of paternal abuse and childhood victimization. Today we are surrounded by powerful cultural forces that impede recognition of the intersubjective character of social life. These cultural determinants undermine our belief in human interconnectedness, contribute to our resistance to thinking intersubjectively, and provide Ms. A. and others with the means to resist both personal and social relatedness. This anti-intersubjective predisposition of our cultural universe contributes, I will argue, to a particular form of self-structuring and self-formation.

In suggesting an answer to the question of why Ms. A. attempted to present herself as a hopeless victim of parental abuse rather than as a free, unencumbered moral agent willingly embracing a relationship with me (and with her

father), we begin to see what is at stake in the current
controversies about trauma and abuse, and in the ideology
of victimization. And when we consider the strength of the
cultural forces that encourage individual selves to identify
themselves as discrete and as unconnected to those around
them—and even to disconnect their minds from their own
bodies—we can understand how difficult it is to resist those
cultural constructions. In the following chapter I will elaborate on these contemporary contexts in which remembering occurs.

2

Memory's Contexts

Ms. A.'s case documents the plasticity of memory. In its demonstration of memory's malleability, it fits with current scholarship—in fields as diverse as the humanities and the neurosciences—on the reality of memory distortion and the capacity of memory to be manipulated.[1] But beyond that, the case allows us to consider a question that has received far less sustained study: What meaning does memory serve? Through Ms. A.'s case we can explore the remembering process: the complicated relation between the individual and the collective, and the ways in which the cultural and the interpersonal interpenetrate in memory, a process generally thought to be purely individual.

I employ this most personal of relationships—between analyst and patient—not as a way to solve the riddle of memory but as a way of exploring its complexity. The questions I asked myself during my work with Ms. A., I now draw on as I reconsider the topic of memory and investigate the ways in which memories are not so much the product of an individual mind as the result of an individual's relation both to self and to the outside world. I call this quality the intersubjectiveness of memory, and I develop an argument that challenges the conventional conception of memory as the product of an isolated mind.

For this reason, I resist treating Ms. A.'s case as part of the conventional psychoanalytic literature concerned with patients who develop a belief that they were sexually abused as children but who probably were not actually abused. These writings are not uninteresting or unimportant, but their main aim is to document the distortions of memory, not memory's meaning. As an example, consider an article published in 1991 by the psychoanalyst Leonard Shengold. Entitled "A Variety of Narcissistic Pathology Stemming from Parental Weakness," it describes a series of cases that conform to the pattern of "false memories."

This article followed by two years Shengold's book *Soul Murder: The Effects of Childhood Abuse and Deprivation.*[2] In the book Shengold considers the lasting effects of actual trauma suffered by children at the hands of adults, which he calls "soul murder." He describes the enduring fantasies generated by the trauma, fantasies characterized by both sadomasochism and rage. He notes the intense psychological splitting that typically occurs, generating extreme obsessive-compulsive mechanisms designed to ward off feelings of inner chaos, and the feeling of being one step removed from one's own life. All in all, Shengold describes results that are typically catastrophic: unconscious fantasies generated by trauma transform the world into a largely hostile and unlivable environment, and the sufferers are barely able to tolerate this world that, in some sense, they have created.

But in the subsequent article Shengold turns to a different phenomenon: patients who came to him, often because they knew of his previous work, convinced that they had been sexually abused and asking for his help in searching for corroborating memories. In these cases Shengold concludes that no trauma occurred, and he attempts to explain why some persons search for memories of abuse that did not occur. In describing these cases, he concludes that each patient had "weak parents," parents largely unwilling and unable to contain their children's intense feelings. As a result the children became adults with an overabundance of fantasies of rage and sexuality, never having successfully contained them as they were growing up. In Shengold's words: "The rage at the unfulfilled promise of 'everything' [a consequence of parents' inability to say no] was disguised and displaced onto various exaggerated charges of mistreatment and misunderstanding directed toward the parents (frequently alongside a defensive idealization of them)."[3]

Ms. A. may well have conformed to this pattern. Ms. A.'s father, who quietly and dutifully acquiesced in his wife's insistence that he be ostracized from the family, may have been an ineffective paternal figure. And even more telling, his response to Ms. A.'s charges of childhood molestation reveals an inability to resist his child's aggression and hostility. Instead he capitulated to it; one might even say he embraced it.[4]

On a number of occasions during Ms. A.'s analysis she expressed enormous rage and talked about her desire to kill me. This murderous rage, and its opposite, her frequent fantasies about leaving the analysis and never coming back, conform to the dynamic described by Shengold: the persistence of powerful fantasies of entitlement and rage that were never structured or dissipated through equally powerful parental containment. Although Ms. A. often engaged in defensive maneuvers to keep such fantasies out of conscious awareness so as to disable her capacity to function effectively in the world, she did eventually let the fantasies surface and become part of our analytic work together, allowing greater integration of her self.

In 1994 David Raphling, also a practicing psychoanalyst, published a clinical report entitled "A Patient Who Was Not Sexually Abused." Raphling introduces his case material by describing what seemed to him to be a disproportionately large number of patients who, either during their treatment or in their initial evaluation, claimed to have been victims of sexual abuse in childhood. These were patients who, according to Raphling, did not exhibit the symptoms most often associated with those who have suffered early trauma. While Shengold was interested in specifying the "environmental pathologies"—that is, parental weaknesses—Raphling focuses more on the constellation of intrapsychic forces within the patient that might generate fantasies of abuse.

In the case he describes, Raphling places oedipal conflicts at center stage: "The notion that one is an innocent victim who has been egregiously and dreadfully wronged is a seductive fantasy that offers gratification of forbidden incestuous wishes while exempting the victim from the personal responsibility that activates superego pressures, cumbersome defenses, and unpleasurable affects."[5] Raphling's patient (whom he calls Miss A.) is a young woman who, much like my own Ms. A., developed the belief that she had been sexually abused at a time in her analysis when eroticized transference feelings were intensifying.

The fantasy of abuse, Raphling argues, was a defensive maneuver to ward off the eroticization of the analytic relationship: "The dynamic function of Miss A.'s belief that she was sexually abused was to deny in fantasy the disappointment of her oedipal wishes. The fantasy that ultimately appeared in her claim of sexual trauma was a compromise that both defended against depressive affect and destructive aggression related to oedipal disappointment, and satisfied superego demands for punishment for her unacknowledged incestuous wishes."[6] Miss A. attempted to fend off what seemed to be intolerable fantasies of aggression and sexuality by creating external conditions that would warrant the intensity of her feelings, feelings that could then be both directed at and derived from a real external object.

These two articles express mainstream perspectives within psychoanalysis. Shengold uses an object relations schema to understand the etiology of individual fantasies, and Raphling employs a classical intrapsychic model to account for similar psychodynamic phenomena. Both reveal an orientation to human experience—a psychoanalytic one—that concentrates on the vicissitudes of human subjectivity, and on the powerful role that unconscious fantasy can play in insisting that reality conform to its image. The case of Ms. A., I believe, corroborates this view and demonstrates, again, the way the psyche can make its own independent contribution to "objective reality."

But with regard to the issue of childhood sexual abuse, it is precisely this exclusive focus on the subjective elements—an individual's encounter with his or her fantasies and internalized objects—that has given psychoanalysis a tarnished image. It has generated the accusation that psychoanalysts refuse to acknowledge the reality of trauma and abuse, preferring to focus on the fantasy of rape, say, rather than on the devastating psychological consequences of being raped.

Psychoanalysis's putative refusal to be sufficiently concerned with real trauma and real abuse prompted Judith Herman, a feminist, a psychiatrist, and the author of *Trauma and Recovery*, to proclaim: "Out of the ruins of the traumatic theory of hysteria, Freud created psychoanalysis. The dominant psychological theory of the next century was founded in the denial of women's reality."[7] Even some practitioners of psychoanalysis have criticized the field for ignoring real trauma in favor of the exploration of unconscious fantasy. Bennett Simon, a psychoanalyst on the faculty of Harvard Medical School, has noted that, until recently, consideration of trauma and abuse has been nearly absent from the psychoanalytic literature.[8]

In that spirit of criticism, the case of Ms. A., along with the articles by Shengold and Raphling, may be seen as further evidence of psychoanalytic skepticism about real trauma and abuse. Psychoanalysts' caution may be perceived as yet another example of their preoccupation with the strange and unpredictable world of the imagination and their concomitant tendency to ignore more obvious and apparent sources of psychological distress.

To be sure, one result of the theoretical concern of psychoanalysis with the role of fantasy and the autonomous role of the psyche—certainly among Freud's most important contributions to the understanding of the individual—has been a general lack of sustained interest in real, "objective" circumstances, at least to judge by the literature.[9] Psychoanalytic writings have concentrated on unconscious fantasy and the ways it interferes with an individual's ability to be free of symptoms or of pathology. And because of this theoretical preoccupation, very little attention has been paid to the ways in which the analyst and patient contribute to analytic productions—the *decision* that childhood abuse, say, defines current psychological difficulties, or that sexual trauma does not figure in the patient's past.

So, for example, David Raphling, in the article discussed above, does not share with the reader how he came to believe that Miss A., despite her own conviction that she had been abused, had in fact fantasized the abuse. Similarly, Leonard Shengold does not tell us how he arrived at the conclusion that in the cases described in his article, in contrast to those described in *Soul Murder,* the patients only *sought* to see themselves as victims of abuse and in fact had not been physically abused. An important intersubjective process between analyst and patient occurred in these cases, producing in each analyst a conviction that no abuse had occurred. But in their presentation the process was hidden from view and the patients themselves were objectified. The patients were portrayed as possessing certain properties—a kind of symptomatology—that explained this phenomenon of imagined abuse. In both articles the mind of the analyst seems to play only a minor role in this process: the analyst is treated as a clinical detail, necessary for the accomplishment of the work but seemingly irrelevant to an understanding of how it was determined that no real abuse had occurred.

But we know, nonetheless, that the analysts were far more central to these dynamics than the authors report: Dr. Shengold acknowledges that many patients enter treatment with him because of his *Soul Murder* book and are searching for memories of abuse in their own pasts; Dr. Raphling expresses his growing concern about the number of patients in his practice who suspect that they were abused in childhood. Clearly these facts influenced the process through which the patients' memory productions were generated, treated, and evaluated, but in neither article do we learn the site-specific, embedded, interactional practices and processes through which knowledge of the past was evaluated, processed, and integrated into the analytic relationship. Nor do we discover how "genuine" knowledge of the past was distinguished from fantasy. We can safely conclude, I believe, that neither Dr. Raphling or Dr. Shengold dismissed out of hand the possibility that abuse had occurred in childhood. But neither analyst spends much time discussing the emergent processes through which the mind of the analyst and the subjectivity of the patient encountered each other, or how they together produced an understanding of and in the patient that did not feature abuse as a central dynamic.

The conclusions drawn by these analysts, in short, surely derived not from a metapsychological predisposition to doubt the reality of abuse but, rather, from an intersubjective exchange that produced in both analyst and patient (though not necessarily simultaneously) a more-or-less definitive understanding of what about the past could be reliably assumed, what remained problematic, and what, in all likelihood, was a product of fantasy. And certainly these are not the only questions to be asked when considering the patient's encounter with his or her past. What is registered as memorable, what is retained, and what is reactivated through the recovery process all help the analyst achieve a deeper understanding of the mind of the patient. This is what animates my consideration of memory: how the remembering process itself, in the present, influences *what* past is remembered. This critical question, raised for me by the case of Ms. A., has not received the attention it deserves.

Today, the past has achieved a kind of iconic, even sacred status. Remembering the past is now widely understood as a valuable activity in and of itself; so much so that how and why we remember in the present is a topic of relatively little popular interest. We tend not to question certain presumptions that elevate *what* is remembered to a powerful place in our symbolic universe. We are inclined not to challenge the determinativeness and significance of the past for the present; and we do not doubt that memory recovery often plays a certain transformative, redemptive role in the lives of those who remember. We have become a society of "memory groups," where one's claim to group membership typically goes unchallenged because a common past, common experiences, or common traumas, now remembered, constitute an area of discourse that cannot be contested. The past, because we hold it sacred, is an extremely powerful weapon, wielded in various ways to generate various kinds of personal and political attachments to groups, movements, and causes. When the past is invoked as the basis for group membership—whether through a shared memory of the experience of immigration, or an identification with those who have suffered past racial oppression, or even a common history of alcohol abuse—the group's reason for being and the individual's identification with it are presumed to be self-evident.

Once memories are introduced into public discourse, either in reference to an individual's past or to a group's, we tend to shift our attention back in time: to leave the present and to focus on how the past shaped, or influenced, the person doing the remembering. Freud's continuing contribution to contemporary cultural life, his emphasis on the past's enduring influence on the present, may be gauged by our predilection to defer to what is claimed to have come before.

Yet as features of our past have become identified as ever more critical in understanding our present, the *process* of remembering has become overshadowed by *what* is remembered. As our interest in the past has intensified, memory itself has been categorized as merely an unproblematic vehicle for reclaiming the past: remembering, as a human and therefore fallible feature of our existence, has not been the object of much critical investigation.

The Remembering Self

The American sociologist George Herbert Mead wrote that the past is an expression of the present, and the French sociologist Maurice Halbwachs wrote that "the past is not preserved, but is reconstructed on the basis of the present." Halbwachs is best known for his interest in "socializing" memory, his efforts to demonstrate the "social frameworks" in which memory necessarily occurs. In an essay entitled "The Social Frameworks of Memory," he says this:

> One is rather astonished when reading psychological treatises that deal with memory to find that people are considered there as isolated beings. These make it appear that to understand our mental operations, we need to stick to individuals and first of all, to divide all the bonds

which attach individuals to the society of their fellows. Yet it is in society that people normally acquire their memories. It is also in society that they recall, reorganize, and localize their memories.[10]

Halbwachs is recognized as the great theorist of "collective memory," a student of Durkheim who set out to de-individualize the study of memory. Since Halbwachs, sociologists have come to appreciate the important contribution of collective symbols, rites, and commemorations to the construction of memory.[11] Moreover, researchers have demonstrated the ways in which the ritual practices of commemorating the past are simultaneously commentaries on the present, responses to present-day concerns in which the past is reinterpreted and re-remembered from one generation to the next.

The case of Ms. A. directs us to a different question, one inspired by Mead and Halbwachs: how in-the-present interpersonal relations and social and cultural contexts are generative and constitutive of what we experience as memories. Freud is often credited with demonstrating the persistent role that the past plays in the unconscious life of the individual; my intent is to invert Freud's original insight and to explore the roles present-day consciousness and current interactions with others play in producing an individual's memories. The case of Ms. A. redirects attention not to the memory of experience but rather to the experience of memory. In this I am charting a distinctively new path for memory studies.

I do acknowledge, as sociologists have already done, the present's influence on the past. This sociological tradition, in effect, insists that memory and temporality cannot be conveniently detached from each other. When we remember and with whom and for what purpose contribute to *what* we remember. But the sociological focus on the rituals, rites, and commemorations of the present—collective symbols—yields insufficient attention to the interpreting self. The self, I argue, is driven by internal pressures to remember the past in the idiosyncratic ways that are required for one to situate oneself temporally in a past, a present, and a future.

Memory's Embeddedness

The details I have provided of Ms. A.'s misremembering over the course of her analysis help us appreciate important truths about memory and the intersection it represents both socially, between the individual who remembers it and the larger world, and temporally, between the here and now when remembering occurs and the layers of remembered pasts inscribed "objectively," though impermanently, in the mind of the present-day rememberer.

Memory is produced by an individual, but it is always produced in relation to the larger interpersonal and cultural world in which that individual lives. The reconstruction of the past always depends on frames of meaning and contexts of significance generated in the present. Memorial productions are inseparable from the socially and culturally located individual, who is intersubjectively linked to the world of others and to a world defined by interpretive cultural frames that connect each person to the larger cultural whole. Memory is *embedded:* that is, the rememberer remembers in a contemporary world, peopled by others who collectively contribute to the construction of memory and help determine the importance that the past holds for an individual in the present.

The case of Ms. A. demonstrates the complex and subtle relation between the rememberer and the surrounding world: there is little doubt that the frameworks through which Ms. A. remembered were those presented by the world her adult self inhabited. These categories of meaning, socially and culturally constructed, helped to determine the past's significance. In short, what we remember of our personal pasts in this particular day, age, and cultural context is different from what we might have remembered of our own pasts at another time or in another cultural milieu. Remembering, while it demarcates our idiosyncratic experiences from those of others, also locates us within a present-day social world.

Memory is embedded because the self is a "socially constructed" or "socially constituted" entity. The self, while experienced as individually created—as if it begins from the inside and moves outward—is in fact unavoidably a historical product of a particular social world. This is a world of other subjectivities that not only tolerate and support the illusion of individual autonomy but insist upon it. The self, experienced as a product of a unique past that uniquely propels it toward the future, is a special feature of the cultural world in which we live.

The philosopher Charles Taylor details the culturally specific, Western understanding of the self that we share, an understanding forged in the modern era. In *The Sources of the Self: The Making of the Modern Identity,* Taylor identifies the Western self as the locus of personal attention, as self-interpreting, and as its own agent of activity. It is a concept that has been forged over the last several hundred years.

Rather than affirming the commonsense and culturally bounded idea of the self as transcendent, standing above social and cultural particularity, Taylor demonstrates that the very idea of the self's transcendent features is a result of the particular quadrants of temporality and sociality in which that self is defined.

Ms. A.'s remembering of childhood abuse cannot be easily disentangled from the "social" discovery of childhood abuse and recovered memory that was going on at the time. In forceful, dramatic, and seemingly legitimate ways, the idea was continually being presented—in books, in the broadcast media, in private conversations—that childhood trauma could be recalled after being out of conscious awareness for years. Ms. A. was undergoing psychoanalysis in the late 1980s, when there was a "sexual abuse movement" in American society identifying childhood traumas, such as incest, as the source of much adult grief and suffering. In 1986 Diana Russell published a book entitled *The Secret Trauma: Incest in the Lives of Girls and Women.* Using a survey of 930 women randomly selected in the San Francisco area, she found that 28 percent had experienced sexual abuse before the age of fourteen and that 12 percent had been victims of incest. These were dramatic and shocking findings; the book, and the conclusions drawn from it, figured prominently in shaping public discussions about the prevalence of childhood abuse.[12]

In due time the U.S. government took special notice of the problem of abuse. The United States Advisory Board on Child Abuse and Neglect was created under the auspices of the Department of Health and Human Services to serve as a factfinder and to make policy recommendations to minimize the occurrence of abuse. This board estimated that, because of the heightened sensitivity to abuse of children, authorities had been able to substantiate the occurrence of more than 500,000 cases of sexual abuse between 1990 and 1995. Some authorities concluded that more than 3 million physical attacks on children occurred during the same period.[13] This dramatic increase in the reporting of childhood abuse was clearly a response to the greater public attention it was receiving and to the realization that almost anyone could abuse a child. Academics, social service professionals, lawyers, and legislators took action to ensure that child abuse would be reported when it occurred, that accusers would be both protected and encouraged to come forward with their accusations, and that the accused, if convicted, would be severely punished for their crimes.

How potent this discovery of rampant abuse of children was at the time can be measured by the extent to which it became a national preoccupation, spawning many stories in the media and spurring many institutions to tackle the problem. The intensity and extent of this preoccupation, which dominated newspapers, television and radio news, and talk shows, strongly suggests that it revealed profound social anxieties of which attention to the problem of child abuse became the visible manifestation.

Indeed, some reactions to the problem reached hysterical proportions: it seemed that the demonstration of the nation's determination not to tolerate child abuse was overwhelming the concern for due process and equal protection under the law. Beginning with the case of the McMartin Center in Manhattan Beach, California, in which members of the McMartin family and others were accused of widespread, frequent, and horrible forms of sexual molestation of children in their care, the nation was racked by such accusations. And though the evidence often was less than compelling and in some cases was nonexistent, many adults were convicted of and imprisoned for abuse of children.[14] A movement begun to protect the rights of children, to uncover mistreatment of children that had been hidden within the family and overlooked by an insufficiently attentive legal and social service system, developed into a full-scale assault on the capacities and willingness of adults to exploit and abuse children, on the institutions created to care for children, and even on the society that tolerated institutions, such as daycare centers, that fostered such mistreatment.

The nation is still struggling to find a way to protect those who have been abused, to prevent future abuse, and to provide mechanisms to ensure that when abuse occurs it is punished while simultaneously ensuring that individuals are not falsely accused, that accusations are not improperly obtained, and that strict standards of proof are not abrogated. For example, the recognition that children are suggestible and that improper questioning can elicit false accusations has meant that much greater attention is now paid to the interrogation of children, in an attempt to ensure that only the truth is elicited.

But despite this more sophisticated effort to combat child abuse while protecting against false accusation, at the time of my work with Ms. A. child abuse in America was developing into a powerful cultural trope, existing independently of the phenomenon itself. Child abuse had quickly become a cultural category, infused by fantasy-based—sometimes delusional—formulations of adult misbehavior. So powerful was this obsession that it was seemingly immune to rational discourse. There emerged an externalized representation of victimizers and victims whose relation to the actuality of abuse sometimes proved to be tenuous at best.

For example, accompanying the discussion of how the nation fails to protect its children were vivid descriptions of satanic cults that included, as part of their ritualized worship, the abuse and sacrifice of children.[15] These tales, never substantiated but never thoroughly discounted, were woven into one narrative after another describing adults' depravity and parents' capacity for criminal behavior. Each story apparently served a need to characterize the society through a representation of absolute and naive innocence—children—overwhelmed by organized forces of unmitigated evil. The cultural critic Marina Warner has written, "incest, molestation and even rape in families has always taken place, but never have more attempts been made—often with appalling clumsiness—to save children from their violators." And the social psychologist Carol Tavris comments:

> Today, we are in the midst of national hysteria about child sexual abuse. As with all moral panics, it stems from legitimate worries—in this case, about the safety of children in our hypersexualized age. And it stems from the understandable rage produced by sensationalized stories of sexual predators and psychopaths. But pedophiles and sexual psychopaths have always been with us. What distinguishes a moral panic from reasoned efforts to deal with sex offenders has to do with the tone and sweep of the solutions offered.[16]

In short, the discourse about child abuse has taken on a

life of its own. The challenge is to distinguish between a belief that abuse is widespread, a scenario in which opportunistic adults are imagined as routinely gratifying their basest passions by victimizing children—a powerful myth that has the capacity to transform inner experience to conform to this externalized category—and the reality of abuse, which in fact is experienced by all too many children. To be sure, given the prevalence of childhood abuse, Ms. A. might have been an abuse victim. But the national preoccupation with the themes of childhood abuse and victimization and Ms. A.'s receptivity to those themes influenced her psychoanalysis. The atmosphere was such that few people would not wonder whether they themselves, as children, had suffered abuse by an adult. The cultural milieu, I believe, was contributing to Ms. A.'s memories.

The "discovery" of repressed memory—adults recovering memories of childhood sexual abuse, sometimes after years of not remembering—came shortly after the public began to think seriously about child abuse. And like the interest in abuse, repressed memory developed into a social phenomenon in its own right and came to assume a cultural significance and meaning more potent than the reality itself. The insistence that repressed memories could be recovered reflected other cultural themes, and became part of a movement critical of the existing society. Women who came forward with memories of abuse participated in a movement that asserted women's entitlement to full self-expression and fought against the repression of one's own memories, against a psychotherapeutic establishment skeptical of the truth of those memories, and against the oppression of a patriarchal society intent on protecting the mostly male perpetrators from the mostly female victims.

These cultural currents fueled the discovery and the believ-ability of recovered memories of childhood trauma.

In *The Courage to Heal: A Guide to Women Survivors of Child Sexual Abuse*, the authors write:

> Often the knowledge that you were abused starts with a tiny feeling, an intuition. It's important to trust that inner voice and work from there. Assume your feelings are valid. So far, no one we've talked to thought she might have been abused, and then later discovered that she hadn't been. The progression always goes the other way, from suspicion to confirmation. If you think you were abused and your life shows the symptoms, then you were.[17]

The possibility of recovering repressed memories encour-aged the search for long-forgotten experiences of child-hood sexual trauma, such as incest, that could help explain current unhappiness or adult dysfunction. In some cases, it seemed, the atmosphere that was supportive of such memories yielded their discovery. There are thousands upon thousands of individuals today who testify that they have recovered their earlier memories and who now iden-tify themselves as "survivors" struggling to overcome the effects of sexual abuse. But, as Carol Tavris points out in the *New York Times Book Review*, a "sex-abuse industry" has been created that includes a tremendous body of literature meant to help people remember earlier abuse and to sur-vive the memories, and a burgeoning army of therapists whose patients consist largely of those rememberers. This industry not only aids those who were abused as children, Tavris notes, but, in addition, has *created* victims, "to expand the market that can be treated with therapy and self-help books."[18]

And this phenomenon has also created thousands of other victims: people, usually parents, who claim to have been accused by their children of crimes that never occurred. The False Memory Syndrome Foundation has been established, with thousands of members—academics, professionals, and lay people—who challenge the legitimacy, at least in some cases, of repressed memory and "recovered memory therapy." The Foundation reports that as many as 15,000 families have contacted it, claiming to be what Mark Pendergrast has described as "victims of memories." In June 1994 the American Medical Association declared that it "considers recovered memories of childhood sexual abuse to be of uncertain authenticity which should be subject to external verification. The use of recovered memories is fraught with problems of potential misapplication." Indeed, pressure is mounting to establish the false memory syndrome as a verifiable personality disorder that, like post-traumatic stress disorders, is subject to diagnosis and treatment.[19]

The pendulum, at least for the moment, is swinging against those who assert the veracity of such dramatic repressed memories, and a challenge is now being made against the idea of repressed memory itself: the idea that traumatic experiences can be forgotten for years at a time, then be recovered with photographic accuracy.[20] Indeed, because of the work of organizations like the False Memory Syndrome Foundation, there is an increasing recognition that some therapists and some accusers have taken advantage of the moment by generating clearly false accusations. Even in newer editions of the sacred texts of repressed memory like *The Courage to Heal,* the authors counsel against too readily following a therapist's suggestions that abuse may have occurred.

When the phenomenon of repressed memory first made its impact, many state legislatures were quick to change the laws, extending the statute of limitations for certain kinds of crimes and certain cases in order to accommodate those who had recovered memories. Now some of those laws have been rescinded, and other states are considering legal changes more carefully. A bill has recently been introduced into the New Hampshire legislature requiring that patients be informed of the experimental nature, the risks, and the limitations of Recovered Memory Therapy. Not long ago individuals were imprisoned as a result of accusations based on recovered memory.[21] Now, juries are finding against such accusations and against therapists charged with improperly implanting the suggestion of childhood abuse in their patients. In California in 1994, for example, Gary Ramona won a $500,000 judgment against a therapist, a psychiatrist, and a hospital for their role in "implanting" a memory of molestation in his daughter. The pendulum has swung so far, in fact, that some observers now argue that the controversy about the dubious claims generated by recovered memory threatens to weaken society's focus on real incidents of childhood abuse and trauma.

Ms. A.'s effort, during her analysis, to align herself with the widely publicized movement of "abuse survivors" reveals the ways in which the organization of an individual's memory is necessarily "contaminated" by social processes. Ms. A. seemed to welcome the chance to identify herself as a victim of abuse, or, to borrow a word from the sociologist Erving Goffman, to mortify herself.[22] For a self racked by conflicting impulses, identifying an external villain as the cause of the internal conflicts may bring a painful pleasure. The prominence of the "survivors" movement encouraged Ms. A. both to identify herself as someone who had been victimized and to seek relief from her suffering by aligning herself with a social world of which she could feel a part.

The social embeddedness of memory accounts for the volatility of Ms. A.'s memorial productions. Viewing memory as socially embedded rightly directs our attention away from exclusive consideration of the individual properties of the mind—the human capacities both to remember and to forget—that enable memory. Focusing solely on memory as a cognitive achievement and identifying the properties of the brain that enable memory to occur, in the end, overemphasizes the isolation of the individual in social life. The individual's embeddedness in the social world contributes in critical ways to the production of memories.

Henri Bergson, the great philosopher of memory, writes in *Matter and Memory* that memory "is just the intersection of mind and matter."[23] For Ms. A., the culturally prominent categories of childhood trauma and abuse and the ready availability of narratives of victimization to account for current pain served, for a time, as material or external resources through which she could recover a past and seek its meaning. As a corrective to the individualized view of memory, I emphasize Ms. A.'s involvement with the socially constituted frames of perception, categories of meaning, and narrative forms through which she came to experience her past and understand her present. Viewing memory as the intersection between cultural *explanada* and mental experience allows us to explore the intersection of the material reality of the external world with the inner world of the mind. I do not dispute the devastating and lasting psychological impact of childhood trauma and abuse, or the heuristic effects of remembering. But trauma and abuse are now presented as a culturally available "narrative package" through which memory can be recovered.

If our brain is the hardware and our past is the data we seek to access through memory, the language of victimization has become a very popular piece of mental software. Without some software package, we could not translate our individual pasts into meaningful language. Ms. A.'s misremembering reminds us not only of memory's malleability but also of its culturally constructed character. The different memories she produced during her psychoanalysis illustrate the connection between memory and the search for a language in which to express, as best we can, our felt experience.

Embodied Memory

Memory not only is embedded in the social universe that helps shape it: it is *embodied* in a particular person, a person actively engaged in forging selfhood. The socially constructed self is situated through a community of others: family, friends, ethnic and other groups, cultural understandings, and so forth. But a constructed self requires an active agent—a person—who does the constructing. Charles Taylor has written: "We can't effectively exercise subjectivity, and be aware of a world, without a sense of ourselves as embodied subjects; for this sense is constitutive of our awareness."[24] Memory is a vehicle by which the embodied self situates itself in the present by reference to its unique past. If we place the individual who interprets and acts upon his or her world—the self as agent—at the center of memory, we assign more importance to the process of recovering memory than to what is remembered. Remembering is a way by which the agentic self constitutes itself in time. It therefore is forged in response to the contemporary needs, desires, and understandings of the remembering self. Without memory to represent the past from which one came, it is impossible to represent one's self as moving through time into the future.

But what does memory represent? The memories one produces are narrative fragments intended to account for one's feelings and bodily sensations—to explain happiness and pleasure, for example, or sadness or feelings of emptiness. These experiences of the self—feelings and somatic states—are a form of self-knowing, largely inarticulate, that often generate a desire for articulation and explanation. The world is made sensible by these embodied "background understandings."[25] Remembering is a response to a desire to articulate this inner world, which is often the site of suffering. It is a process by which a person seeks to reconcile these inner states with outer experience and to situate the painful present in relation to a comprehensible past. A self must develop a particular understanding of its relation to its own person and must actively work to uphold that understanding. The concept of memory as a vehicle of the embodied self helps to explain its volatility: as self-conceptions change, the representations of the past also change to support new self-understandings.

Ms. A. was trying to find a language to account for her own self-experience. During her psychoanalysis she was unhappy, depressed, and desperate to relieve the suffering.

These were the feelings that brought her into treatment and that motivated her to explore her past and its relation to her current state of being. It would be callous to suggest that her misremembering was, in any sense, willful deception. Through the analysis, she was trying her best to articulate what I call the *embodiment* of her experience, her background understanding of herself and the world whose source was not in the present but inscribed from the past. These current feelings are inherited from the past—a past in which prior experiences and relationships have been processed and encoded, generating fantasies, in some instances, of well-being, and in others, of deprivation, frustration, and need.

In this respect, the motivation to remember requires no pressure from the surrounding culture. Feeling states, sometimes clearly understood by the interpreting self but sometimes inchoate, exert their own internal pressure to be represented, interpreted, and acted upon. Whereas considering memory's *embeddedness* encourages us to pay attention to the influence of the present on the recovery of the past, considering memory's *embodiedness* directs our attention to the ways in which feeling states and bodily desires, inherited from the past but prevailing in the present, can rewrite the past in the service of the present. The need to remember can overwhelm history itself: the aspiration to achieve certain feeling states, or to dispel others, generates fantasy, imagination, and reconstruction that amount to a reinvention of the past.

To illustrate the conception of memory as embedded and embodied, suppose that, rather than focusing on the question that has dominated memory studies, namely memory's relation to history, we pose other questions. Does imagining (or wishing) oneself to be, for example, an "abuse survivor" affect what part of the past one remembers, and what meaning one assigns to it? How does the anticipation of assuming a particular social role, one that carries a host of meanings and significance, shape the memory of past experiences? How may knowing that child abuse is widespread and that it is not uncommon to repress trauma—the stuff of popular discourse—affect what one remembers, and what one takes the memories to mean? Questions about the interpersonal and sociocultural context in which memory occurs and the effects of the desire to find explanations in the past for current feeling states have not been sufficiently considered in efforts to make sense of the debate over recovered memory.

I believe that this more complex conception of memory will better illuminate, for example, what occurred in Ms. A.'s analysis than will an exclusive focus on a conception of the past driving the present. Let us move away from Ms. A. for the moment and consider another case of a young woman of today "recovering" long-repressed memories of childhood incest. Perhaps the best-known and best-publicized case is that of Eileen Franklin Lipsker. Her case is so well known because it was one of the first cases of recovered memory to result in court proceedings against the accused, because in it the link between childhood trauma and repressed memories was first legally argued, and because of the horror of the memories she recovered. Her accusations resulted in a life sentence for her father.

The case was brought to public attention by Lenore Terr, a psychiatrist who testified at the trial, and whose work has focused on the lasting effects of childhood trauma on its victims. In Terr's *Unchained Memories* she describes how, twenty years after the events, Eileen Lipsker came to recover memories of being raped by her father, of being raped by her godfather with her father's participation, and of witnessing the rape and murder of a young friend, Susan Nason. The murder was part of the public record and until that time had remained unsolved. Terr relates the process by which Eileen slowly recovered more and more of these memories: "One recollection, however, led to another. Over the next several months, many small bits of Eileen's memory returned. Some were sights, a few were sounds, and some were simply thoughts. Eileen Lipsker found herself inundated with a slow, but inevitable memory cascade."[26] As a result of Eileen's accusations her father was charged with abuse of his daughter and with the murder of Susan Nason. Though no material evidence was produced, he was convicted on the basis of Eileen's recovered memories and sentenced to life in prison. Later, however, key witnesses, including his wife, retracted their testimony, and he was released.

The details of this case have been the basis of challenges to repressed memory therapy, attacking it for its failure to recognize that memory can be a product of suggestion.[27] Critics have offered alternative explanations for Eileen's recovered memories, and have demonstrated that the supposed facts of the case do not stand up to close investigation. They have asserted that the recovered memories of Eileen and other patients are in fact false memories generated by inappropriate suggestions made by their therapists.

But the reasons, or motivation, behind Eileen Lipsker's recovery of memory have been largely uninvestigated. Why, we might ask, would Eileen be willing, after all those years, to reveal those memories, particularly if they were false ones, but even if they were genuine? Laying claim to those memories, despite their horror, must have contributed to a conception of herself that was far more appealing to her than the one she held before she produced the memories. Her memories, when recovered, gave her a new and more vivid sense of herself. They also gave her a closer relationship with supporters of repressed memory therapy, who had been suggesting, directly or indirectly, that the recovery of memories represented the pathway to recovery and cure.[28]

In remembering, this young woman (and others like her) is surely engaged in a profound realignment between a present self and the past, and striving for a different, perhaps more authentic-feeling, relationship with key participants in that past. But the remembering surely also restructures her current relationships with herself and with others—with her family members, with her therapist, with members of a group involved in memory recovery, with a movement in which childhood abuse becomes a source of meaning and identity. We may imagine this young woman now organizing and situating her life in the context of those memories of the past: the memories may provide a vitality of experience and a principle of self-organization she has long sought but never attained or sustained. Moreover, her relationship with those she has accused is probably irretrievably altered, replaced by an adversarial one. This change occurs whether her memory is accurate or is a conscious or unconscious confabulation. For the rememberer, the consequences of remembering are in many respects independent of past events. The rememberer's present-day motivations for remembering can hardly be separated from the memory itself: through memory, the past, present, and future converge.

The psychologist Elizabeth Loftus, who is internationally renowned for her research in the psychology of memory, over the past several years has become an outspoken opponent of the concept of repressed memory, and often testifies against repressed memory therapy. She is on the Scientific and Advisory Board of the False Memory Syndrome Foundation. She and Lenore Terr frequently find themselves on opposing sides of court battles between recovered memory plaintiffs and accused defendants. In her book *The Myth of Repressed Memory* Loftus demonstrates that it is possible to implant false memories of childhood events. And she shows that, once implanted, these memories can come to be experienced by the rememberer as real.[29]

Loftus describes the case of Chris, a fourteen-year-old boy, who was asked to read descriptions of four incidents that had happened in his childhood. These accounts were written by his older brother, an undergraduate working in Loftus's laboratory. Three of the four events had actually occurred, but the fourth was a fabricated story about Chris, at the age of five, getting lost in a shopping mall and, after some time had passed, being reunited with his frantic family with the help of an elderly man. Loftus tells us that Chris, in subsequent weeks, appropriated this false memory as his own; in fact, in describing the fictitious event himself, he added details. He described, for example, the plaid shirt the man wore and the pipe he was smoking. Loftus offers this, along with other cases, to demonstrate the human capacity to misremember.

The sequel to the story of Chris is even more interesting, and, for my purposes, more telling. At the end of the experiment Loftus "debriefed" Chris, explaining the purpose of the experiment. And, because of the sensitive character of the research, she discussed it with him again six months later. Each time, Chris heard that the mall incident had never really happened, that it had been planted to explore some ideas important in memory research. Chris assured Loftus that he understood the explanation. Some months later a local television station reported on Loftus's research, and Chris was interviewed. In the interview he said something like this: Professor Loftus has told me that my getting lost in the mall never really happened, and so has my older brother, but it still feels real to me.[30]

Why, we might ask, did Chris insist on preserving the memory, even knowing that both Professor Loftus and his brother said the event had not happened? This characteristic of memory seems to me especially interesting, for here Chris's memory seems to be driven by present-day needs and desires clearly having nothing to do with the incident itself or the supposed trauma suffered at the time. We do not have enough information to know precisely why Chris chose to preserve this memory, but a few possibilities come to mind. Perhaps Chris was responding to a deeply felt need, one we probably all share, to provide a coherent and consistent account of himself as a self, one whose memory serves adequately to situate him in relation to his past and continuous with it. To disown the story, after having affirmed and even embroidered it, might have threatened Chris's sense of self and the work he had put into achieving it.

If we consider the story itself, a tale of the triumph of reunion and reconciliation over feelings of traumatic loss and abandonment, we can imagine the reluctance one might have to disown it. It is a powerfully gratifying account in which forceful and conflicting emotions are engaged and childhood fears are responded to—we might say contained—by an avuncular man and a distraught family. For Chris this emotionally engaging tale may well have captured some of the unconscious, elemental dynamics of family life: his striving for autonomy and independence, his fear of his own assertive impulses, and his wish for a family forgiving and accepting of those impulses. But for Chris this life narrative—whatever the particular psychological reasons—was too pleasing to resist. Loftus presented the case of Chris to prove the malleability of memory and the unreliability of the mind in the reconstruction of the past, but the sequel to the story illustrates, beyond that, the way social and personal coordinates in the present generate and sustain particular stories of the past. Seeing memories in this way, as narratives intended to recapture the past or as categories of self-understanding, gives reason to their unreliability.

Memory and Self-Constitution

To recapitulate, memory is intersubjectively constituted. While memory is produced by an individual, what is remembered is always influenced by the cultural world in which the individual is embedded. It is important to consider the potent effects on memory of the interpersonal world, the psychodynamic, typically unconscious forces that give it meaning, the more distal cultural frames or categories of perception, and the accompanying narratives of experience available for "meaning-making." Memory is also motivated by the individual's relation to his or her own feeling states. This, I argue, constitutes the inscription of the past into the present. Memory, in this sense, is an effort to reconcile self-understanding or self-consciousness with one's inner world of feeling.

At the same time, neither the concept of memory as embodied nor that of memory as embedded fully captures the remembering experience. After all, the apparently intense psychodynamic, interpersonal, and cultural pressures to understand herself as an "abuse survivor" that were enveloping our work together, did not, in the end, overwhelm Ms. A.'s capacity to know for herself what had occurred earlier in her life and to understand its relation to the present. Together we were able to find our bearings, to resist the temptation to use external abuse to explain her current difficulties. In spite of the appeal of that explanation, we found our way to a more internally based understanding of the sources of her unhappiness.

The outcome expresses the limitations of a sociology of memory that fails to include a conception of mediating selves capable of resisting dominant cultural modes of thinking. The self, able to symbolically mediate between possibilities and to exercise (when the conditions are right) reasoned and reflective judgment, is the third important factor in this consideration of memory. But we should not be too sanguine about the role of the self. Recall that Ms. A.'s memories of abuse, too, were products, in part, of her relationship with me and her attempts to protect herself from me. Here we encounter clearly and directly the conflict-ridden nature of the self. Her memories of abuse in early childhood constituted an effort to defend against the perils of a self whose feelings at the time were too intense and/or too dependent.

When Ms. A. and I began her analysis together, we defined our work as "returning to the scene of the crime," as reconstructing the childhood experiences and understandings that continued to hold sway in her adult life. We shared the psychoanalytic axiom that to treat the painfulness of the present it is necessary to rediscover the past. But by the end we shared an appreciation of the greater complexity of the analytic process; we understood the interpenetration that occurs between the past and the present as well as the permeability of the boundaries between memory and the wider social world, the world that offers markers directing us toward what to remember. We better comprehended both how her experiences in the present were shaped by frames of meaning and barriers of defense determined earlier and how her search for understanding and meaning in the present created an unstable past, one forever subject to reinterpretation.

This is the central thesis of this book. Memory, viewed as a process of remembering, necessarily constitutes and reconstitutes relationships, including one's relationship to oneself. Memory establishes a framework of understanding by which the rememberer constitutes himself or herself as occupying a specific place at a particular time, always in relation to others and to a past as well as a future. Memory is not the only dimension of self-constitution, of course, but it is surely crucial for situating oneself both socially and temporally. The construction of a self depends upon our capacity to provide a coherent, consistent, cohesive, continuity-producing account that, partly by reference to the past, locates us meaningfully in the present: situated in relation to ourselves and to others, and poised to reckon with the future.[31]

No one captures this dimension of memory and the purpose it serves better than the neurologist Oliver Sacks, when he describes his patient Jimmie, who lost all short-term memory. Sacks asks: "But were there depths of this unmemoried man, depths of an abiding feeling and thinking, or had he been reduced to a sort of Humean drivel, a mere succession of unrelated impressions and events?" And he responds to his own question: "Jimmie both was and wasn't aware of this deep, tragic loss in himself, loss *of* himself. (If a man has lost a leg or an eye, he knows he has lost a leg or an eye; but if he has lost a self—himself—he cannot know it, because he is no longer there to know it."[32]

Mental health clinicians are well aware of how variable the past can be: of how powerfully attitudes toward significant people, and concomitant memories about them, can change over the course of a patient's therapy. As Israel Rosenfield argues, "not only can there be no such thing as a memory without there being consciousness, but consciousness and memory are in a certain sense inseparable, and understanding one requires understanding the other."[33] Yet neither those who endorse the idea of recovered memory nor those who challenge it acknowledge that memory is always mediated through an interpreting self engaged in a present-day, interpersonally embedded process of remembering, and driven, too, by bodily states of being. Rather, the proponents and opponents of recovered memory share a presumption about the objectivity of the historical past.

For example, advocates of repressed memory like Lenore Terr insist that an individual's recollection of past events sometimes requires the intervention of therapists or others, to assist in removing what can be formidable barriers of repression: defense mechanisms unconsciously designed to protect the individual from reexperiencing, that is, from affectively remembering, earlier traumas. According to this rendering, memory—what really happened—is inscribed as a permanent record in the brain, but sometimes the mind attempts to deny the person access to these memories because of the intolerable emotions with which they are associated.

Those who challenge the phenomenon of repression, like Elizabeth Loftus, understand memory as malleable and unreliable, vulnerable to the distorting influence of suggestion. Loftus's impressive corpus of research supports these claims concerning memory's malleability. But while these critics of repressed memory are less likely to think of experience as inscribed in the brain like a permanent record, they do focus largely on ways in which memories can be manipulated or distorted by improper suggestion or false presumption about the past. It is important to note that both camps view history as recoverable—under optimal conditions—by the *individual.*

Memory, in short, is conventionally understood as quintessentially an individual attribute, separate from the social and cultural world in which the individual is embedded and from the feeling, sensate body that "houses" the individual, or the self. For those who believe in repressed memory, "true" recollection of past trauma requires social intervention to overcome an individual's tendency to deny an unpleasant or painful past. The critics of repressed memory, meanwhile, argue that memory easily succumbs to outside intervention, producing recollections of events that never occurred. Yet in both cases the conviction is that

individual memory and social frames of meaning and signification—social determinations in the present—stand
apart from each other.

The alternative view of memory that I propose in this
book admittedly—in our context and in our time—swims
against the tide. I view memory as necessarily intersubjective. The tendency to individualize memory, to view it as
a record of a historical, real past and to isolate it from other
mental and sensate functions, expresses, I believe, the
alienated character of present-day thought. Alienation or
self-estrangement is the hallmark of both social and scientific discourse today, and one result is the kind of polarized thinking about the individual that the current debate
over memory expresses. The contemporary preoccupation
with history as determinative of memory is but one expression of this form of estrangement. Furthermore, the biological body—in particular, the brain—is understood as
the site in which memory functions; neuroscience has
emerged as the obvious domain in which to resolve the
questions that memory raises. By insisting on the objectivity of the past, memory studies concentrate on the problem
of distortion and have generated intense scientific controversy. But when memory is understood as a vehicle of self-
constitution, it cannot be examined without an investigation of the contexts in which it occurs.

In the rest of this book I will present an account and a
critique of these alienative ways of thinking. I will offer, in
their place, an alternative conception of memory, one that
places the rememberer squarely in the middle of a world
of people and things, engaged in a continuing effort—
sometimes conscious, often unconscious—to reconcile the
inner world with a perceived external reality.

3

Memory, Culture, and the Self

The debate over memory centers on what the psychoanalysts Robert Stolorow and George Atwood have called a central organizing myth of Western culture: "the myth of the isolated individual mind."[1] This myth generates the presumption that each individual possesses his or her own record of what has happened in the past. What undermines "accurate" memory in this rendering is either distortion of the past by intrapsychic processes or fallacious remembering as a result of contemporary external influences.

A scientist presuming that the mind is isolated might be interested, for example, in investigating the capacity to remember accurately; indeed, there is a substantial research tradition that begins with this premise. In this tradition, much work has been done on the psychological phenomena of repression and dissociation, two mental mechanisms that seem critical to the process by which the past becomes distorted or forgotten. These psychological processes in which painful or difficult experiences are either split off from conscious self-awareness (dissociation) or consciously forgotten (repression) are studied for their role in creating "the reality of illusory memories."[2]

Another rich body of research explores ways in which the mind is subject to distortion through suggestion.[3] Both of these research orientations begin with the premise of the discrete individual who, for various reasons, is sometimes simply not up to the task of differentiating truth from distortion. This view of the individual mind as isolated is what ensures that the contemporary debate over repressed memory remains at an impasse, highly politicized and, in these terms, irresolvable: while putatively about memory, the debate is really about the nature and character of the individual. Do individuals unconsciously fool themselves about the past, or are they susceptible to influence by others? What on the face of it appears as scientific controversy in fact expresses fundamental moral uncertainties about the strength and capacity of the individual person to know for himself or herself.

But in identifying this mythical dimension of the Western belief in the isolated mind, Stolorow and Atwood note an alternative perspective, what they call the "intersubjective foundations of psychological life." They suggest exploring the nature and consequences of the mutuality between individuals and the outside world. This points toward a distinctively different orientation to personal and social life and to the individual. In developing the implications of this new orientation, it is possible to offer new questions that better explain the controversy over memory, and that provide a route of scientific inquiry that avoids the current impasse.

This intersubjective perspective is explicitly intended to situate the individual within a broader social framework;

the person is understood as constituted through his or her involvement with others similarly constituted. As conceived in this way, remembering occurs not *in* the individual but intersubjectively *through* the social environment in which the individual is embedded. Through encounters with this broader world, from which frames of meaning and understanding come to be applied to their own feelings and experiences, individuals establish themselves as participating social members and as meaningfully connected to others.

Intersubjectivity, in Stolorow and Atwood's words, "brings to focus *both* the individual's world of inner experience *and* its embeddedness with other such worlds in a continual flow of reciprocal mutual influence."[4] By emphasizing the relation between the individual and others, the concept of intersubjectivity offers an alternative to a conception of memory in which the present is understood exclusively in relation to a determinative past. The process of remembering is now appreciated for its relation to the social world in which it occurs, and as making its own independent contribution to what is remembered, distinct from past events or experiences. This emphasis on the mutuality of the individual and the embedding world distinguishes the intersubjective from a more conventional perspective emphasizing memory either as a mirror reflection of an individual's past or as vulnerable to efforts by others (for example, overly eager therapists) to plant suggestions and generate distortions.

If Stolorow and Atwood seek to de-isolate the person by embedding him or her in a broader world of other persons and a larger cultural universe, the sociologist Anthony Giddens offers a complementary critique of the social world, rejecting a conception of it as isolated from the world of individuals. As individuals become formed by relating to the world beyond themselves, so too does a stable, predictable social world depend upon individuals acting meaningfully toward it. Rejecting a dualism that considers social institutions and structures of society to be objective and pitted against the subjectivity of the individual mind, Giddens proposes his own form of intersubjectivity—what he calls "structuration theory"—and argues that "structure is both the medium and the outcome of the human activities which it recursively organizes."[5]

Whereas psychological intersubjectivists seek to socialize the individual agent, sociologists like Giddens are now involved in "subjectivizing" the social world and overcoming the view of human beings and societies as discrete. Giddens conceptualizes the role of subjectivity in the constitution of society. In his view, the self is constructed through individual interaction in a proximate world of people and things and, in addition, through more distal patterns of symbolic and cultural signification, mediated through an interpreting self.

A full appreciation of the intersubjective world in which we live suggests an even more profound critique of contemporary views than those made by either Stolorow and Atwood or Giddens. If the conception of the individual as an isolated entity expresses a contemporary denial of the intersubjective character of social life, a conception of the brain as isolated from the body in which it is housed similarly denies the mutuality of mind and body. In current neuroscientific efforts to understand memory distortion, the remembering brain has become a focus of attention, as if its properties might stand apart from the body that "motivates" remembering. The move toward a neurobiological reduc-

tionism in memory studies—the scientific aspiration to discover the isolated properties of the brain that result in true
or false memories—is the mirror image of the proclivity to
isolate the individual person from the larger and constitutive social world. I will return to these themes shortly.

A focus on intersubjectivity constitutes a radical critique
not only of the isolated individual who remembers alone
but also of the disembodied mind or brain that remembers
only truthfully or falsely. The case of Ms. A. both documents the power of contemporary denials of intersubjectivity and describes the social setting that encouraged us to
think of the memories she produced as both unembedded
and disembodied. As we originally conceived our work
together, Ms. A. was working hard to uncover her own
private secrets—to exercise her memory muscle—so that
the past might yield up the sources of her present pain.
The fluidity of her memory suggests the danger of down-
grading memory to a mere mental function or structure,
overlooking an appreciation of its productive, contemporary, and interpersonal features.

The case of Ms. A. thus points up the need for an elaborated and more robust conception of the self, one that we
arrived at through the course of our work together: an
agent continually negotiating mind with body, individual
with social world. In this chapter I offer a theoretical
defense of the position I first adopted clinically: that memory is both embedded and embodied, and that it is constitutive of the remembering self.

Self-Consciousness and Alienation

The concept of intersubjectivity represents a significant
epistemological break with conventional understandings

about the present and its relation to the past, about the subjective world of individuals and the objective world of people and things that putatively exists independently of the individuals. And while this perspective defies the Cartesian duality of self and other, of an unbridgeable division between objectivity and subjectivity, it derives from another respected lineage in Western philosophy. Hegel, in particular, challenges this dualism and offers in its place a theory of intersubjectivity. Hegel considers the problem of self-consciousness and the nature of individual experience, starting with the synchronic connection between self and other at any given time in history. The implications of Hegel's thinking for distinguishing memory from a history that is remembered are significant.

Hegel and later Marx believed in a knowable and meaningful "movement of history": that we are all unwitting participants in history's progression toward its final destination. Because of their teleology, the importance of their social and psychological analysis has been largely disregarded. Nonetheless, their insistence on the inextricable connection between subjectivity and the objective world, and their argument that the appearance of separation between the two is the phenomenal manifestation and production of alienation, can provide a framework for understanding the consequences of a culture that both rejects an interconnectedness of the individual and others and conceives of the individual mind as isolated from the surrounding world.

In sum, the intersubjective tradition, forged by Hegel and Marx and organized around the centrality of individual alienation, remains central to an understanding of the world. By providing a theoretical context for interpreting the myth of the isolated mind, intersubjectivity gives us a way to understand the contemporary propensity to collapse the distinction between memory and history, or to eliminate the distance between the subjective process of remembering and the objectivity of the history being remembered.[6]

As Edward Hundert explains it, "What Kant overlooked [but Hegel noted] is that *we* (and our mental faculties) are, like the objects we experience, also in the world. Our nature (including our faculty of reason) is as much a 'contingent' fact of the existing world as anything, and as the world changes so must our conception of it."[7] The link between the development of self-consciousness and an unfolding history distinguishes Hegelian philosophy from its Anglo-American counterparts, for it dialectically connects the individual mind, manifested concretely in historically specific moments of partial self-awareness, with the universal movement of history toward freedom, or full self-consciousness. The universal can be realized, Hegel argues, only through individual consciousness; the two cannot be conceived except as mutually interconnected.

In *The Phenomenology of Spirit* Hegel takes up the problem of recollection, or memory, at the end of history, that is, "Spirit's triumphant self-absorption." In the end of history, Richard Terdiman writes, "what we remember is the other made ours—an epiphany reassuringly harmonizing self and world, past and present, being and becoming."[8] Yet until that epiphany is achieved, memory and history are not synonymous. The Spirit is manifest in (incomplete) self-consciousness and represents simultaneously the incorporation of the past and its transcendence. Memory is the human being's interpretation of the past, not its recapturing; it is the production of the past, not its excavation.

Identifying the achievement of full self-consciousness as history's ultimate project, Hegel systematically develops an individual psychology. His theory of the dialectical relation of the individual to a situated, embedded social world distinguishes him from those, like Durkheim and Bourdieu, who see the individual person as the carrier of the past, almost as identical to it.

Hegel's theory of individual psychology corresponds to his division of the world into its manifest concrete expression and its universal, transcendent essence of which the concrete expression is an incomplete articulation. In Hegel's account, the development of the individual begins with a stage of complete self-absorption, with little recognition of an outside world; the child has no conception of universal humanity, abstract and external. As the youth acquires ideals, ambitions, and hopes, the dialectic unfolds: fuller self-consciousness becomes possible, and over the life course, the isolated subjectivity of the individual comes to be mediated through the objective reality of the external world. Jerrold Seigel summarizes Hegel's developmental psychology: "Maturity rested on 'recognizing the objective necessity and reasonableness of the world as he finds it—a world no longer incomplete, but able in the work which it collectively achieves to afford the individual a place and a security for his performance. By his share in this collective work he first really is *somebody* gaining an effective existence and an objective value.'"[9]

Healthy individuals are characterized by their capacity to embody in their private selves all of reality that extends beyond them, experiencing themselves as part of or as connected to the surrounding world. Insanity is "a state in which the mind is shut up within itself, has sunk into itself, whose peculiarity consists in its being no longer in *immediate contact* with actuality but in having positively *separated itself* from it." Seigel restates Hegel's formulation this way: "Engrossed in itself, the mind in a state of disease was unable to recognize its relation to the outside world, and suffered from the contradiction between external reality and 'the single phase or fixed idea' that ruled within." Hegel argues that "man alone has the capacity of grasping himself in this complete *abstraction* of the 'I.' This is why he has, so to speak, the privilege of folly and madness."[10]

Here, for Hegel, is the ever-developing relationship between self-consciousness and unfolding social forms. The self is both the mover and the moved, and self-consciousness expresses the dynamic relation—in the present—between subjectivity and the objective relations in which it is embedded: "For although the world must be recognized as already complete in its essential nature, yet it is not a dead, absolutely inert world, but, like the life-process, a world which perpetually creates itself anew."[11]

The dialectic between subjective existence and objective reality, once in motion, according to Hegel, generates alienation or estrangement. The collectivity is experienced as having no reality in one's own being; it is felt to be apart. Our very categories of understanding express the alienation we experience. These categories include the ways in which we remember or the categories and experiences in the present that motivate and organize "alienated" remembering. Alienation induces in consciousness the conditions or the motivation necessary for its transcendence. Through memory, we seek to overcome alienation; yet, in experiencing remembering as exclusively subjective, we simultaneously *produce* alienation. Our attempts to understand the relation of our past to the present through memory, though appearing to express an exclusively subjective reality, are constituted through categories of understanding generated by the external world.[12] For Hegel, the condition of alienation is what ultimately propels us toward its transcendence, toward the overcoming of the division between subjectivity and objectivity.

No one employed Hegel's ideas more powerfully than Karl Marx. Marx's historical materialism derives from a Hegelian analysis of alienation and its movement toward being overcome. Though Marx, unlike Hegel, characterizes nonalienated labor as the condition of full self-consciousness, he preserves the Hegelian dialectic and the identification of alienation as the force propelling history forward. Perhaps Marx's most compelling critique of capitalist social relations is found in his Early Philosophical Manuscripts and, in particular, his analysis of alienated labor. Alienation, for Marx as for Hegel, expresses the estrangement of the individual from the species. But for Marx the preservation of man's humanness depends on man's ability to reclaim, through active labor, the object world as part of his subjective, lived experience.

In "Alienated Labour" Marx begins with the premise that man in the natural world, dependent upon nature for sustenance, acts upon nature to produce a social world of which he is part. The "sensuous external world," through man's labor, is transformed into a world of objects, an alien world that stands outside and above the subjects who create it. But though created by human activity, the object world gains in prominence and significance, dwarfing the individuals upon whom its existence depends, and making them increasingly dependent on it for their survival. The individual subject becomes increasingly "a slave of the object." This, for Marx, is a necessary human condition, one that he calls alienation: "the worker is related to the *product of his labour* as to an *alien* object."[13]

Yet, Marx reasons, as the person becomes increasingly dominated by the object world, which seems to exist independently of its human creators, human activity, now increasingly defined in terms of objective needs, is alienated from the individual actor. Alienation from the object world yields what Marx calls "self-alienation," the estrangement of the individual from himself. "If the product of labour is alienation, production itself must be active alienation—the alienation of activity and the activity of alienation. The alienation of the object of labour merely summarizes the alienation in the work activity itself."[14] Self-alienation generates its own pathology: as the individual is increasingly required to define himself according to the objective world, the individual also becomes estranged from the species.

The human being, in contrast to animals, produces "when he is free from physical need and only truly produces in freedom from such need." But now, when the objective world of (seeming) necessity thwarts the subjectivity of freedom and consciousness, alienated man, Marx insists, is no different from an animal. Life activity becomes limited to providing for physical existence, and as a result human beings become estranged from those aspects of self which define their humanity. The creation of an externalized, objectified social world, in short, "alienates from man his own body, external nature, his mental life and his *human* life." "A direct consequence of the alienation of man from the product of his labour, from his life activity, and from his species-life, is that *man is alienated* from other *men*." When Marx writes that "in the relationship of alienated labour every man regards other men according to the standards and relationships in which he finds himself," he argues that the experience of individuals as isolated from one another is a product of the condition of alienation. Because of alienation, the interconnected, mutually constitutive worlds of self and others are perceived as separate and apart.[15]

What Marx offers is a theory of intersubjectivity. He provides a history of its development both from the perspective of the subject, who becomes alienated from others and the object world, and from that of the external world, which influences subjectivity. Marx, like Hegel, captures the intersubjective and reciprocal character of social life, and analyzes the alienated life that promotes the denial of interrelationship.

Alienation is the consequence of a social world that culturally, theoretically, and epistemologically denies the intersubjective foundations of both individual and collective life. In *Contexts of Being: The Intersubjective Foundations of Psychological Life*, Stolorow and Atwood identify distinct dimensions of alienation; each dimension, they argue, is a consequence of the prevalence of the myth of the individual isolated mind.[16] They describe, first, an alienation from nature, in which an individual subject (the mind) becomes differentiated from physical, organic nature (the body) and either denies vulnerability to impersonal natural processes (of mortality, for example) or reduces subjectivity to something akin to "pure physicality." In either of these forms, a dialectical interchange between mind and body is absent and therefore genuine subjectivity is impaired. And in both cases these alienated responses constitute defensive denials of human vulnerability and mortality.

They describe next an alienation from social life, in which the mind as a separate entity generates an experience of aloneness. It is this phenomenon that corresponds most closely to the popular usage of the term alienation, a condition that has been portrayed by some of the greatest writers in our culture. Stolorow and Atwood argue that the illusions of self-sufficiency and autonomy serve "to disavow the intolerable vulnerability of the very structure of psychological life to interpersonal events over which the individual has only limited control."[17]

Finally, Stolorow and Atwood describe an alienation from subjectivity, in which the mind itself is experienced materially, as if it, like the body, is simply part of a physical reality over which the person has little or no control: "In a culture of pervasive psychological aloneness, there is little to protect a person from feeling that the solidity of things is dissolving into thin air." Here, Stolorow and Atwood echo Marx and Engels's famous lines in the *Manifesto of the Communist Party:* "All that is solid melts into air, all that is holy is profaned, and man is at last compelled to face with sober senses, his real conditions of life and his relations with his kind."[18]

But Stolorow and Atwood rely too heavily on "the cultural myth of the isolated, individual mind" as the force generating psychological alienation. In offering a cultural explanation for alienation, they are not wrong. By describing human beings' embeddedness in a larger social universe, they draw attention to the fact that the *appearance* of individuality and freedom both masks and expresses people's sociability and the external sources of constraint. They describe the ways in which an individual's social embeddedness generates a personal conviction of the separation between mind and body, and of the isolation of individual from individual.

Social embeddedness, as I have argued, rightfully directs our attention away from exclusive consideration of the individual properties of the mind that make memory possible. Focusing solely on memory as a cognitive achievement and attempting to identify the properties or structures of the brain that enable memory to occur, for example, overemphasizes the isolation of the individual in social life and ignores the critical role of social embeddedness in the production of memories. Considerable research, much of it in evolutionary biology, has documented ways in which the social world alters brain structure and function (see Chapter 5). The relationships between the individual and the society and the past and the memory of it are not simple unmediated ones; rather, they are complex, moving back and forth between self and other, between the past and its memory. A personal past and the social world that enables it are inseparable: a theory of intersubjectivity lets us consider how we remember what happened in the past as a part of the larger issue of how our understanding of our own subjective experience is socially constructed and organized.

But recognition of the embeddedness of individual life in a social universe is not enough to allow us to understand how memory is distinct from the history being remembered. When Stolorow and Atwood point to the "cultural myth" as the culprit in fostering alienation, they depreciate the role of a mediating self in generating the conditions for its own alienation. The concept of social embeddedness directs our attention to the ways in which categories of understanding and codes of meaning reflect back upon the individuals who attempt to situate themselves socially and temporally in the world; it encourages us to consider how we employ these frames of meaning to make sense of our life experience. Thinking of the individual as socially embedded emphasizes social consciousness, that is, the way individuals structure themselves through mechanisms provided by the broader social world.

In focusing on embeddedness we should not overlook the conflicts that occur within the self as the person seeks to reconcile sociability with desire. Cultural formations are also inscribed or encoded internally.[19] These feeling states, sometimes clearly understood by the interpreting self, other times more inchoate, provide their own pressure, clamoring to be represented, interpreted, and acted upon. In my view, feeling states express a personal history, in which earlier experiences and meanings drawn from them have been inscribed unconsciously, in a way that appears to be physical. A person carries himself or herself according to a life-long accumulation of experience. Charles Taylor offers an example of this form of embodiment:

My sense of myself, of the footing I am on with others, is in large part also embodied. The deference I owe you is carried in the distance I stand from you, in the way I fall silent when you start to speak, in the way I hold myself in your presence. Alternatively, the sense I have of my own importance is carried in the way I swagger. Indeed, some of the most pervasive features of my attitude to the world and to others is encoded in the way I project myself in public space; whether I am macho, or timid, or eager to please, or calm and unflappable . . . This understanding is not, or only imperfectly, captured in our representations. It is carried in patterns of appropriate action, which conform to a sense of what is fitting and right.[20]

The concept of embodiment implies not only the internalization of a history of cultural forms of social stratification but also an individual who possesses a unique set of past experiences *and* a unique history of interpreting and inscribing experiences, which cumulatively form current self-understanding and give the individual a sense of what is fitting and right. Marx, more than Stolorow and Atwood, directs our attention to the ways in which individuals actively generate their own alienation "from the inside." This is what I describe as the *embodiment* of social life— social life encoded in inner experience—which makes its own independent contribution to estrangement. Such an elaborated conception of subjectivity is a contribution of psychoanalysis to intersubjectivity. It goes beyond the perspective of Stolorow and Atwood, who propose intersubjective foundations for psychological life but do not develop its implications for an agentic self that must mediate between its felt experience and the world in which it is embedded.

I will consider two manifestations of embodiment—sexuality and the aspiration to reconcile external reality with inner need and desire. I believe that these dimensions of subjectivity contribute to an understanding of memory and generate a radical rethinking of the relation of the present to the remembered past. The need to remember can over-whelm history itself: the aspiration to express certain feeling states, or to achieve or dispel others, may bring into play fantasy, imagination, and reconstruction that are hardly synonymous with the past.

Synchrony and the Self

Robert Jay Lifton, in *The Protean Self*, describes "the self," "one's inclusive sense (or symbolization) of one's own being," as a key agent, different from the biological person and mediating between the worlds of subjectivity and objectivity. Lifton, in appreciating that the self is "enor-mously sensitive to the flow of history," captures the way in which this mental structure of selfhood acts, interpreting the external cultural and symbolic worlds, and reflecting back on the person as an "independent" causative agent. The self, he says, is "an engine of symbolization as it con-tinuously receives, re-creates, and extends all that it encounters . . . with symbolization, no relationship, idea, impulse, or blend of any of these is immune from modifi-cation or recombination. As a result, the self's belief and value orientations can become 'like particles in moder-nity's accelerator.'"[21]

Lifton invokes the work of Suzanne Langer on "symbolic forms" and Ernst Cassirer on "symbolic transformations" to argue for the creative role of the self in bridging the inner and outer worlds of experience, as an "open system" continually negotiating the individual's encounter with external reality. "Rather than the classical psychoanalytic concept of symbol making as a primitive, unconscious mechanism involving one thing standing for another," Lifton writes, "symbolization in this broader view becomes the all-encompassing mode of self-function."[22]

The self, in short, navigates the world of personhood with other people and things. It interprets the world and acts back upon the subject. Lifton emphasizes this continued interchange between a constituted self, engaged in the world around it, and an ever-changing environment in which the individual is embedded. The result, as Lifton describes it, is a process in which bodily needs and social experience become calibrated in the individual—a continual dance of reconciliation between the expressiveness of the body and the evolving way in which it is represented socially.

Lifton's conception of a relational self, synchronically mediating between bodily sensation and social experience, is reminiscent of the work of Maurice Merleau-Ponty, the French phenomenologist who engaged in a spirited defense of Freudian psychoanalysis and contributed to what has been described as an existential psychoanalysis. In a chapter entitled "The Body in Its Sexual Being" from *Phenomenology of Perception*, Merleau-Ponty rejects a conception of human sexuality as fully explicable biologically, but rather identifies sexuality as an expression of the meaningfulness of all bodily experience within the web of social life. Affectivity or emotional states, he says, have typically been understood as sealed within an individual body, unmediated by others. But he argues that human emotional life is "shot through with intelligence." He means that affect can be represented by the individual or externalized into other people and things. Affectivity is a unique form of consciousness, where emotional life is projected outward into a sexualized world.[23]

Understood in this manner, sexuality is not a "bodily function" or an "involuntary action" but is suffused with intentionality that "follows the general flow of existence and yields to its movements." Sexuality describes an individual's relation to existence—"a manner of being in the physical and inter-human world." "But . . . the body does not constantly express the modalities of existence in the way that stripes indicate rank, or a house number a house: the sign here does not only convey its significance, it is filled with it." "Neither body *nor existence* can be regarded as the original of the human being, since they presuppose each other, and because the body is solidified or generalized existence, and existence a perpetual incarnation." Body and existence then constitute a form of "inter-communication," each dependent upon the other, coexisting temporally, a dialectic of the self and the other that delineates the intersubjectively constituted human world.[24]

Sexuality, it might be said, is a contemporary expression of inscribed, or embodied, past experiences and relationships and fantasies about past and future ones. It constitutes a form of memory that is intrinsic to self-understanding but, because it is felt or appears only as bodily sensation, largely cannot be contained through narrative, an "unrepresented affective state."[25] As Merleau-Ponty argues, sexuality, being "shot through with intelligence," serves as a repository for the past in the present; the erotics of contemporary experience denote the continuing influence of a unique past on the present, a past that seeks in the present its expression and gratification. Thus sexuality is one form of the intrusion of a deeply layered and largely unintelligible and uninterpretable past that insists on being acknowledged in the present.

Freud's description of the centrality of infantile sexuality is his way of understanding how the world of mutuality, that is, the relation between infant and mother, is organized and interpreted by the infant. In specifying this libidinal zone, Freud was intent on establishing the meaningfulness of early life, its organization around zones of pleasure for the infant, and the potency of unconscious experience in influencing perception and other conscious activities from then on.

Subsequent object relations theorists identify in the first encounters of the infant with the mother's breast the basis of sexual or libidinal pleasures. The baby's satisfaction from its mother's milk holds physiological significance, what Freud would call the gratification of self-preservative instincts. But the infant also fantasizes the absence of mother's milk, in the form of the lost object—the mother's breast. And from that primal experience, psychoanalysts argue, both sides of the duality of existence—self-preservation instincts and sexual ones—become inscribed in the infant's subjective world. The fantasy of breast is simultaneously the fantasy of physical satiation and the imagination of pleasure restored.

These analysts reject a purely biological view of early sexuality and identify the critical role of the "other" in shaping, organizing, and ultimately articulating it. In this view, sexuality is socially communicated, principally through preverbal mechanisms. Nancy Chodorow, in her important work *The Reproduction of Mothering*, makes this point powerfully: "Women, as mothers, produce daughters with mothering capacities and the desire to mother."[26]

As Chodorow makes clear, this process of socialization is not restricted to a cognitive understanding of the importance of identification and role-modeling but also involves deep psychological communication in which female desire expresses itself through nurturing. While desire is universal and transcultural, Chodorow argues, its satisfaction through female nurturing is a culturally specific artifact, reproduced in each generation by mothers who organize sexual experience in their daughters by a nurturing "impulse." What distinguishes Chodorow and other object relations theorists from proponents of a biologically driven model of sexuality is their emphasis on the ways in which sexuality becomes socially communicated and organized— in extraordinarily subtle and nuanced ways, largely inaccessible to conscious knowing. While sexuality's origins are interpersonal, its experience becomes inscribed internally.

The neo-Lacanian Philippe Van Haute characterizes this nonreductive model of sexuality as a consequence of the caregiving relationship that is established from the moment of birth: "In so far as sexuality is introduced in the child in and through the relation of care (that is, in a relation that aims at the satisfaction of the instincts of self-preservation), this new and radicalized model is an intersubjective version of the [Freud's] original theory. Sexuality no longer just 'emerges' in the child, but it is rather introduced into the child from the outside."[27] Parents, largely unknowingly, express toward their children their own socially constituted sexuality and inscribe it on them.

The embodiment of a sexualized past requires constant negotiation by a self attempting to mediate sexual expression in a world of others, a world that demands impressive sexual and interpersonal constraint. The British psychoanalyst D. W. Winnicott best captures this realm of experience, which he calls the third dimension of life that exists between inner reality and the external world. He systematizes Merleau-Ponty's insight about the dialectics of self-constitution by offering a depth-psychological and developmental account of how the individual, in early life, develops the capacity to mediate between bodily experience, such as sexual desire, and the limits and constraints imposed by others.

Winnicott explains psychoanalytically the paradox of a self that reflects upon itself simultaneously as the creator of the external world and as a consequence of it. In his most important essay, "Transitional Objects and Transitional Phenomena," Winnicott writes: "The third part of the life of a human being, a part that we cannot ignore, is an intermediate area of *experiencing*, to which inner reality and external life both contribute. It is an area that is not challenged, because no claim is made on its behalf except that it shall exist as a resting-place for the individual engaged in the perpetual human task of keeping inner and outer reality separate yet interrelated."[28] In this essay Winnicott explores the relationship between an infant and a "transitional object," a teddy bear or other cuddly object that comes to have special meaning and significance to the infant. He argues that the relationship between child and cuddly thing is an illusionary one; the pleasure from the transitional object derives not from the physical sensuality of the teddy bear or even from the companionship it may yield. Rather, the transitional object yields the fantasy of a world under the omnipotent control of the person who has created the illusion that the cuddly object is "something special." Pleasure defines this third dimension of human experience and, once achieved, becomes a feeling state to which all subsequent experience is compared.

The real theoretical advance here is not simply in discovering this intermediate area of experience but in recognizing it as an intersubjective production. Winnicott reasons as follows: Illusion making is not inherent in the individual. Rather, it represents an achievement based upon the presence of an internal object that "is alive and real and good enough (not too persecutory)." The internal object, a concept derived from Melanie Klein, is a mental concept held by the individual of important others, such as his or her mother. "But this internal object," Winnicott says, "depends for its qualities on the existence and aliveness and behaviour of the external other. Failure of the latter in some essential function indirectly leads to deadness or to a persecutory quality of the internal object."[29]

Inner reality, external life, and illusion are dimensions of experience, and the quality of each is inextricably bound up with the others. Absent a "good-enough mother," deprived of an approving and accepting internal object, the individual cannot well tolerate, or derive pleasure from, this intermediate zone of selfhood through which the individual confronts and, later, relates to the world. Even more significant, without these requisites the individual is incapable of mobilizing illusionary experience on behalf of separation from the object. "Of the transitional object," Winnicott writes, "it can be said that it is a matter of agreement between us and the baby that we will never ask the question: 'Did you conceive of this or was it presented to you from without?' The important point is that no decision on this point is expected. The question is not to be formulated."[30]

This illusionary sphere enables the individual to conceive of external reality as if it were of his or her own making, and thus to experience objects independently of the "real" life-sustaining needs they fulfill. At the same time, comprehending the world as if it is of one's own making depends on others facilitating our deception—never asking the question—thereby permitting us to experience our dependent status as autonomy from those objects. This illusion of selfhood, of the individual as agent, allows us to enter the world of shared reality, to participate with others, to derive sustenance from them. In other words, the illusion of autonomy is a condition of our sociality. Anthony Elliott expresses clearly the Winnicottian paradox: "The emergence of a stable core of selfhood, according to Winnicott, depends on establishing the kind of relationship which is at once liberating *and* supportive, creative *and* dependent, defined *and* formless. For it is within this interplay of integration and separation that Winnicott locates the roots of authentic selfhood, creativity, and the process of symbolization, as well as of social relations and culture."[31]

In offering illusion as a third dimension of experience, Winnicott describes the possibility of a mutually constituted, collaborative, and consensually agreed upon cultural fact: social interdependence expressed through the illusion of individual autonomy. He shows how a social life committed to principles of autonomy and self-reliance generates in the individual feelings of well-being and contentment that coincide with society's expectations. In contrast, feelings of dependence, deindividuation, and so forth may be described as pathological feeling states in which the individual experiences himself as discordant with society's expectations. For Winnicott, the illusionary quality of social interaction makes cultural life, predicated on individual autonomy, possible. By agreeing not to ask the question of origins in order to facilitate individual autonomy and independence, the culture turns a blind eye to the dependent and inextricably interconnected nature of human beings.

Christopher Bollas, an interpreter of Winnicott's writings, elaborates on Winnicott's description of the experiencing self. In *Being a Character: Psychoanalysis and Self-Experience*, Bollas characterizes self-experience as the capacity of the individual to derive pleasure and satisfaction from the surrounding world—the world of people and of things. The self, or selves, come to be known to the individual, Bollas writes, only "through problematic encounters with the object world."[32] Through those experiences we produce our own idiomatic and eroticized relation to the world around us, that is, we subjectivize the outside world and make it part of our own unique psychic structure. The outside world leaves its traces within us, and, for Bollas, vitalizing self-experience occurs when inner life and object world resonate with each other.

Together Winnicott and Bollas describe the necessarily intersubjective origins, development, and constitution of the self. More than that, they explode the common wisdom that the self is engaged in a lonely, isolated struggle toward formation and self-definition. Winnicott offers a way to understand the mutuality of self and other in human experience. The development of the self depends upon the establishment and nurturing of the illusion of individual separateness, autonomy, and activity, an illusion fostered by others who, by their constant and nonpersecutory presence, enable it to flourish. Such individuation, in short, is not separate from the simultaneous attachment process that both characterizes self-experience and depends upon it. The mutuality of self and others produces a social field in which the self is able to derive gratification from others, and in which others are enhanced and transformed by creative, loving selves.

From infancy onward the self mediates between the world of what are felt to be inner needs and the shared reality of outer experience: it is creative, in flux, and always in formation. The self, we might say, is the activity through which the individual is always trying to put into form what it believes it needs—coherence, cohesion, consistency—and to reconcile experience with the more-or-less stable, cohesive person encountering it. In contrast to the more classical psychoanalytic language that describes the self or the ego as a psychic structure or apparatus, Winnicott's formulation, like Bollas's, captures the dimension of human agency attempting to accommodate new experience to more-or-less constant, albeit conflicting, inner needs within the available frameworks of self-understanding and self-experience. The self is never static but is always working upon itself, attempting to integrate outer and inner worlds.

Both Winnicott and Bollas conceive of psychopathology as a disease of the self or of human agency.[33] The multiple worlds of experience, inner needs, and shared reality are insufficiently coordinated by the agent of the self. The self has failed to consolidate a centralized, integrated control system mediating among the worlds of feeling, needs, and experiences.

Psychopathology too is intersubjectively caused: usually

by a failure of the interpsychic world of parent and child. As the child develops, under normal circumstances, this process of mediation gains in complexity. For example, a child's capacity to split the world into good and bad, or to distinguish between kinds of experiences, typically deepens over time into an ability to integrate good and bad into a nuanced and ambiguous system of emotional affect and meaning. The competence to coordinate between contending and conflicting forces is an attribute of the self, of agency, a skill that expresses the increasing capacity of the maturing individual to mediate between worlds. It is in this respect that memory becomes ever more important in one's effort to locate oneself coherently in time and in relation to others.

Of course, these skills of coordination and integration are not always up to the challenge. Kurt Fisher and Catherine Ayoub assert, for example, that severe trauma or maltreatment can prevent individuals from developing these mechanisms of coordination: "As children attempt to cope with the extreme dangers of repeated sexual, physical, or emotional abuse, they organize their thought and action in ways that are adaptive in dealing with the abuses, helping them to survive. These patterns can become integrated into the fabric of a child's personality, and then they often prove to be maladaptive for coping with more benign, day-to-day interactions."[34]

If pyschopathology can be understood in terms of failures of the intersubjective world to nourish and sustain the growth of the individual self, situating oneself in relation to one's past—memory—helps one to make one's way in the present. For Bollas, memory is an important dimension of this never-ending search for self-experience, as the individual tailors past events and experiences to meet present-day needs and desires. As Bollas puts it: "Memory becomes a kind of gathering of internal objects, developing an inner constellation of feelings, ideas, past images, body positions, somatic registrations, and so forth that nucleate into a sustained inner form."[35] In placing at the heart of human experience the creation and sustenance of a self-state that locates the individual in his or her social world, Bollas and Winnicott both note that memory of the past is among the resources available to the individual for defining and making vivid the self-in-formation.

The Malleability of Memory

If we think about memory developmentally, it is clear that a conception of what happened in the past and its distinctiveness from what is happening in the present is acquired concurrently with the development of a self. There is a time, early in one's life, when memories of past experiences and a sense of oneself as independent from the surrounding world are extremely weak. Memory and the construction of a self go hand in hand. As Karl Popper and Sir John Eccles put it in *The Self and Its Brain:*

In order to be a self, much has to be learned; especially a sense of time, with oneself extending into the past (at least into "yesterday") and into the future (at least into "tomorrow"). But this involves *theory;* at least in its rudimentary form as an expectation: there is no self without theoretical orientation, but in some primitive space and some primitive time. So the self is, partly, the result of the active exploration of the environment, and of the grasp of a temporal routine, based upon the cycle of day and night.[36]

Having a past theoretically organized as memory is essential to our ability to live in relation to others in the present. The requirement to situate ourselves temporally and in relation to others demands a complexly organized self; in this way, as I have said, memory and the development of the self are concurrent processes. Memory requires a complex self because it involves a subtle interchange between past events, a mental representation of those events, and the application of an interpretative framework. At the same time, without memory, the development of a complex self is impossible. Memory, as Israel Rosenfield has argued, is synonymous with the development of complex self:

> My memory emerges from the relation between my body (more specifically, my bodily sensations at a given moment) and my brain's "image" of my body (an unconscious activity in which the brain creates a constantly changing generalized idea of the body by relating the changes in bodily sensations from moment to moment). It is this relation that creates a sense of self; over time, my body's relation to its surroundings becomes ever more complex and, with it, the nature of myself and of my memories of it deepen and widen, too. When I look at myself in a mirror, my recognition of myself is based on a dynamic and complicated awareness of self, a memory-laden sense of who I am.[37]

Nicholas Humphrey and Daniel Dennett describe the self as rather like "the center of narrative gravity of a set of biographical events and tendencies," or a "fictive self," in which narrative options are continually constructed and evaluated as one forges a dominant understanding of oneself: "In the normal course of development, she [the human being] slowly gets acquainted with the various possibilities of selfhood that 'make sense,' partly through her own observation, partly through outside influence. In most cases a majority view emerges, strongly favoring one version of the 'real me.'" The self, as construction, relies on an understanding of the past so one is able to orient oneself both to the present and the future. As Lifton puts it:

> The symbolizing self centers on its own narrative, on a life story that is itself created and constantly re-created. To be sure, the self can fall from narrative and undergo perceived breaks and radical discontinuities in life story. It can also divide itself into many subnarratives sufficiently developed to form their own self-structures or subselves. The self never stands still: "A so-called steady state . . . is really not a changeless state but a slowly advancing act."[38]

In this process of self-construction, the individual, as Gilles Deleuze says, is simultaneously the inventer and the believer: memories are invented to uphold a particular self-conception and, at the same time, are experienced as incontrovertible truths to which the self must conform. "The subject invents; it is the maker of artifice. Such is the dual power of subjectivity: to believe and to invent, to assume the secret powers and to presuppose abstract or distinct powers." Or, as Christopher Bollas succinctly describes it, the individual "experiences himself both as the arranger of his life, and as the arranged." The individual simultaneously views himself or herself as the creator of his or her experience, as having his or her own stories of one's past, and as subordinate to the theoretical orientations, experienced as commonsense facts, that help him or her remember, that is, interpret and make meaningful, that experience.[39]

But the "stories of one's past" or "theoretical orientations" through which the self comes to be experienced as both the creator of life and created by it are always in flux, "a slowly advancing act." One's self (or even one's selves) is never static, its formation never complete. The reason is simple: the world of people and things through which the self is constituted and reconstituted is itself always changing. The cultural universe through which one's individuality and uniqueness become defined is never in a steady state. New experiences, new relationships, new understandings are forever superimposed upon earlier ones; new dimensions of one's own self are perceived; new memories that help organize changing self-perceptions are elicited. Memory, in short, is part of this unending work of selfhood, of organizing and locating oneself in relation to the cultural language of the cultural universe around one. New theoretical orientations influenced by new encounters and experiences (including psychoanalytic relationships) provide new opportunities to reconcile feeling states with recollections of the past.

Through memory the self attempts to anchor itself in this changing world of people and things. Richard Terdiman, in *Present Past*, tells us that "memory is a theory machine. And theories are memory machines . . . because they determine what, in the flux of experience, we apprehend and cognize. Theories organize what we notice, and thereby what we recall. By determining interpretation they act inevitably as schemata for memory."[40] In sum, the conventional and static understanding of memory cannot be sustained. Indeed, as Terdiman implies, memory is as much an application of what we in the present believe we know to be significant as theory is an expression of the inherited wisdom of what has been deemed significant through time. With respect to the self and the ways in which its needs are met, the present and the past are hardly discrete entities in individual consciousness. They converge through the constitution and continual structuring of the self.

4

Trauma and the Memory Wars

In 1980 the American Psychiatric Association established a new diagnostic category, post-traumatic stress disorder (PTSD). In specifying a unique configuration of symptoms associated with trauma, the APA legitimated what mental health practitioners had long been encountering clinically: veterans of the Vietnam war suffering persistent psychological problems whose origins could be traced to their war experiences. By identifying PTSD as a disorder with a specific etiology and a wide, though clearly demarcated, range of symptoms, the APA grouped under one diagnosis disparate illnesses like shell shock, combat stress, delayed stress syndrome, and traumatic neurosis.

PTSD has aroused extraordinary interest both as an illness and as a research topic. This interest has yielded not only new kinds of treatments for war veterans but also great insight into the diagnosis and treatment of other victims of traumatic stress: airline crash survivors, released hostages, witnesses to violent crimes, and so forth. Cathy

Caruth, the editor of *Trauma: Explorations in Memory,* describes this recent development:

> This [PTSD] classification and its attendant official acknowledgment of a pathology has provided a category of diagnosis so powerful that it has seemed to engulf everything around it: suddenly responses not only to combat and to natural catastrophes but also to rape, child abuse, and a number of other violent occurrences have been understood in terms of PTSD, and diagnoses of some dissociative disorders have also been switched to that of trauma.[1]

Also in 1980, the American Psychiatric Association recognized multiple personality disorder (MPD) as a diagnostic category (now referred to in the *DSM-IV Manual* as dissociative identity disorder). What had been a rather exotic diagnosis, found most often in fictional characters like Dr. Jekyll and Mr. Hyde or Dorian Gray or the title character in *The Three Faces of Eve,* now became part of the real-life diagnostic arsenal of mental health practitioners. They began to discover MPD in more and more of their patients. Some clinicians now confronting MPD suggest that in the past it has often gone undetected, and perhaps been misdiagnosed as schizophrenia, borderline personality, or depressive disorder.[2]

The increased reliance on the diagnosis of MPD has led to the establishment of organizations like the Association for the Study of Dissociation, under whose auspices mental health practitioners, and often their clients as well, convene to discuss current knowledge on the topic and even to celebrate—as a sign of the professional community's developing understanding of the nature of the illness—the dramatic increase in numbers of those diagnosed. But there are significant grounds for concern about this mushrooming of diagnosed cases of MPD. As the researcher Nicholas Spanos puts it:

Modern cases of MPD have tended to take on truly bizarre characteristics. For example, early cases rarely involved more than two or three alter personalities per patient . . . [but] many modern cases involve 20 or more alter personalities per patient, and in some cases the alters number in the hundreds. Child sexual abuse was not a prominent feature of MPD cases reported before 1970. However, cases reported after 1975 have almost always involved descriptions of childhood sexual abuse, and the kinds of abuse purportedly experienced by these patients have grown progressively more lurid and more extensive. Some patients not only report such "conventional" forms of abuse as father-daughter incest but also tell tales of having been subjected to bizarre sexual torture at the hands of secret satanic cultists and of having been forced to endure multiple pregnancies and births only to see their newborn infants torn away and sacrificed at obscene rituals.[3]

What else might be at work here? Both PTSD and MPD are understood to be caused by gross traumatic events such as wartime battles or kidnappings, which occur once or repeatedly, or by overwhelming experiences such as sexual or physical abuse in childhood occurring over a sustained period. These experiences are so profound and so troubling that the individual is unable to assimilate them as part of normal mental functioning: the external trauma wreaks psychological havoc on those traumatized. Thus while PTSD and MPD are distinctly different psychiatric diagnoses, they share common origins in trauma. Both express the incapacity of those traumatized to live normal lives: overpowering external events fail to become integrated within the self; the past never becomes subordinated to the present. Those with MPD or PTSD are ever victims of their memories, haunted by the past. And that past is not of their own making: they are, if you will, victims of history. As Caruth says, "the traumatized . . . carry an impossible history within them, or they become themselves the symptom of a history that they cannot entirely possess."[4]

For Caruth and many others, psychiatry's discovery of the devastating personal consequences of trauma is long overdue. PTSD was a diagnosis forged and refined in treatment of Vietnam war veterans who were clearly traumatized by wartime experiences and, in many cases, incapable of ever fully recovering. The available diagnostic categories were not adequate for those living the aftermath of traumatic war-related experiences. Caruth was a student of Dori Laub, the Yale University psychoanalyst who pioneered psychiatric research on Holocaust survivors by first collecting testimonies of their time in World War II concentration camps. For these trauma victims, too, it is believed that traditional psychiatric diagnoses were inadequate. Those interested in post-traumatic stress have come to use the experiences of war, either by combatants or by concentration camp survivors, as the source material by which to understand the range of symptoms generated by external trauma.

While PTSD requires us to confront a public history of war and genocide, MPD demands that our attention turn to a more intimate but no less horrifying history—often occurring within families—of physical and sexual abuse of children by adults. The presumption here is that psychiatry's recognition of MPD, like that of PTSD, is a response to the reality of a traumatic history and its devastating psychological consequences. The increased reliance on MPD as a diagnostic category has coincided with the growing recognition of the widespread occurrence of child abuse. Contemporary dissociative symptoms, the argument goes, have their origin in this traumatic past, and any reluctance to diagnose the disease implies unwillingness to accept the reality of the offenses.

Yet it seems to me that, as the profession and the society have become more interested in the external world as a cause of disease, we have tended to lose interest in individual persons—their psychological complexity, their capacity for symbolic transformations, even their specific character traits. I believe that the current preoccupation with trauma has resulted in its overuse as a diagnostic tool. It has become the far too clumsy vehicle through which practitioners attempt to understand individual psychology. The pendulum has swung too far away from an appreciation of the extraordinary complexity of individual subjectivity, with a tendency to reduce all understanding of the human psyche to external material conditions that impinge upon the person.

The result is an elaborated social psychology, one that implicates the external world in life's pain and that is sympathetic to individuals innocently caught in the grip of history. This is, to be sure, a way of thinking that is careful to avoid "blaming the victim." But because of this emphasis on the centrality of external events and circumstances to individual psychology, mental health practitioners now find themselves always searching for the traumatic roots of psychopathology. In foregrounding the external world's impact upon the person, we have moved toward an alienated psychology. If wartime experiences or childhood incest cannot be identified in the history of any given patient, we scan for "trauma-like" experiences to account for the patient's psychological distress. Moreover, a discourse has developed that suggests that responsibility for pain and suffering (and, conversely, health and happiness) also lies external to the individual. Behind the attention now paid to trauma is the insistence that we no longer turn a blind eye to the perpetrators' profound and enduring harm to their victims; an unintended result is that we pay less and less attention to psychodynamic processes internal to the individual as sources of psychic suffering.

While many trauma researchers and clinicians insist that current directions in psychiatric diagnosis reflect the profession's genuine encounter with history and society's greater readiness to take responsibility for its toll on individual lives, there is something more at work here. Our tendency to search for a traumatizing past to account for psychological pathology is but a single expression of a broader cultural pattern. Our society is currently involved in an assault on subjectivity itself, eager to replace a focus on the interpretative, meaning-making, symbolizing self with a focus on history and its determinative impact upon individuals.

This process has generated a particular understanding of memory that also emphasizes the effects of the external world—in this instance, "the past" as objectively true—and disputes memory's subjectivity. With our discovery of trauma and our decreasing interest in symbolic mediation, we have been developing a one-sided social psychology: a psychology driven exclusively by the external. As we have adopted an ever more "objectivized" psychology we have simultaneously embraced an ever more robust defense of alienated experience, a conviction that psychiatry must examine the world outside of subjective experience so as to determine its impact on subjectivity. Psychopathology has come to be considered synonymous with an unhappy person victimized by external circumstance.

As component parts of this new social psychology, a triumvirate of concepts make up this alienative vision of the individual as passively reactive to a world largely outside of his or her control. The first of the three concepts is trauma. Our emphasis on the external events happening *to* the individual has made contemporary psychiatry largely identical to traumatology. The study of individual psychology is the study of how the individual's environment defines subjective experience. Typically, when psychiatrists are not being trained in the science of psychopharmacology, that is, biological medicine, they are being instructed in the art of case management, learning to help patients cope with the ways in which the environment overwhelms their capacity to function. In both instances, the external—the biochemical body and the determining social environment—is privileged over the internal, subjectivizing, interpreting self.

The second concept is repression or dissociation, considered to be the person's automatic response to traumatic circumstances. Repression and/or dissociation, it is believed, can be overcome only through memory, just as Freud and Breuer originally argued in their *Studies in Hys-*

teria. Integrating traumatic experience into single consciousness requires remembering the trauma and acknowledging the pain exacted by the traumatic event and, if it is a product of human actions, by its perpetrators. Memory, in this psychology, is appreciated not for its symbolic properties as a *process* of remembering but rather for its capacity to reclaim the past. Memory is considered a vehicle by which what has been forgotten or dissociated from consciousness can be reintegrated.

The third concept making up this newly regnant social psychology is narrative. Traumatic memory—what has been repressed or dissociated—must be transformed into narrative. The individual masters the traumatic experience by narratively mastering an account of it. And while much contemporary work on narrative and narrative theory emphasizes the socially constructed, emergent, and contingent character of the stories we tell, contemporary psychiatry's interest is different. Narrative, one's life story, is a form of externalization, a movement away from the momentary subjective experience toward its disciplining through a recounting of the external events of one's life.

Elaine Showalter has written about "hysterical narratives" or "hystories," a mode of expression that she believes has reached epidemic proportions today. She identifies contemporary cultural narratives about alien abduction, chronic fatigue syndrome, satanic ritual abuse, recovered memory, multiple personality syndrome, and the Gulf War syndrome (one might add post-traumatic stress disorder) as possessing common properties: "Like all narratives, hystories have their own conventions, stereotypes, and structures. Writers inherit common themes, structures, characters, and images; critics call these common elements *intertextuality.*" These "hystories" share a paranoid vision in which various factors outside one's control are identified as resulting in one's victimization. The result of the potency of these tales is the development of somatic symptoms concordant with the narrative, a "protolanguage" in which the symptoms are, in Robert M. Woolsey's words, "a code used by a patient to communicate a message which, for various reasons, cannot be verbalized." As Showalter says:

> We need not assume that patients are either describing an organic disorder or else lying when they present similar narratives of symptoms. Instead, patients learn about diseases from the media, unconsciously develop the symptoms, and then attract media attention in an endless cycle. The human imagination is not infinite, and we are all bombarded by these plot lines every day. Inevitably, we all live out the social stories of our time.[5]

Practitioners of contemporary psychiatry have shown little interest in these questions of the contemporary construction of the tale and its contribution to symptom formation. They focus instead on the story itself, that is, its content. In psychotherapy the patient is instructed simply to reclaim the past, and to integrate it into a single consciousness through narrative. But this leaves the narrator outside the story: it necessarily becomes a tale of the formative circumstances that have created the teller. The goal of therapy, as Pierre Janet expressed it a century ago, is to transform traumatic into narrative memory.

The contemporary celebration of the narrative form—accepting it at face value—and of narration as therapeutic cure underscores the ascendance of this overly socialized and objectivized psychology. Instead of focusing on what narratives of the past reveal about meanings and perceptions in the present, therapists have isolated the narrative from its production. The tendency has been to treat it—when it is offered or recovered through therapy—both as external to the narrator and as revelatory of the historical origins of the narrator's current pain. Narrative, in short, encourages an alienative psychology. The literary critic Mieke Bal has observed: "The narrative text is also an objectification, it is *about* something, someone, that does not participate in the locution . . . And since immediate expression [without narration] is no more possible than access to the image of the self in the mirror, it is also alienation."[6]

The mental health community has been active in promoting this new, antisubjective psychology—thus demonstrating the inevitable connection between scientific practices and broader cultural assumptions that influence the practitioners. The practitioners' favoring of certain diagnostic categories yields the symptoms that are looked for, and encourages patients to feel, subjectively, as the diagnosis implies they will feel. The more frequent diagnosis of MPD, for example, coincided with a growing cultural preoccupation with child abuse; that preoccupation was reinforced by the presence of MPD, and vice versa. The discovery of the high incidence of child abuse provided a way to account for the upsurge in diagnoses of multiple personality and dissociation.

Ian Hacking, in *Rewriting the Soul: Multiple Personality and the Sciences of Memory,* describes the process by which dissociative experiences came to be understood as consequences of abuse in childhood. He begins with a clinical account of multiple personality published in the *International Journal of Psychoanalysis,* in which the psychoanalyst Steven Marmer conjectured that early childhood trauma *might* have contributed to his patient's dissociative symptomatology. From Marmer's carefully documented speculation—never asserting the historical accuracy of the memories—came an increasingly robust insistence in research papers and standard textbooks that sexual trauma *causes* multiple personality. "The linkage between childhood trauma and multiple personality did not emerge slowly over one hundred years," Hacking tells us. "It came into being almost suddenly, in the 1970's . . . Psychiatry did not discover that early and repeated child abuse causes multiple personality. It forged that connection, in the way that a blacksmith turns formless molten metal into tempered steel."[7]

The unfortunate result of this hasty marriage between dissociation and trauma is that etiology and symptom have become inextricably entangled: "A certain picture of origins is imparted to disturbed and unhappy people, who then use it to reorder or reorganize their conception of their past." There may well be a true link between childhood trauma and dissociation. But the assumption that the link exists is undoubtedly culturally generated, a response to motives other than scientific ones. And the assumption is self-fulfilling and culturally reproducing. A patient's suffering of dissociative moments generates a search for a traumatic past; the emphasis on childhood trauma has created the capacity to experience contemporary states of being through the language of dissociation. "We should not think of multiplicity as being strictly caused by child abuse," Hacking explains. "It is rather that the multiple finds or sees the cause of her condition *in what she comes to remember* about her childhood, and is thereby helped. This is passed off as a specific etiology, but what is happening is more extraordinary than that. It is a way of explaining oneself, not by recovering the past, but by redescribing it, rethinking it, refeeling it."[8]

In short, MPD, like PTSD, has provided a kind of guidebook by which the past is interpreted and understood in relation to the present, and a widely accessible language by which contemporary self-experience is described. It captures what Hacking has called "world-making by kind-making," suggesting the important link between available categories of perception and the way individuals describe, think, and feel the past.[9]

The world of a traumatic past is created by an individual who scans for it, organizes a past in relation to it, and comes to feel like a survivor of it. Meaning is given over to the trauma itself. Abuse in childhood is understood as causing dissociation, for example, with no regard for the ways in which individual selves encounter the past, remember it, and constitute themselves in relation to it. Dissociation happens because of the mind's incapacity to absorb overwhelming experience: it is outside the individual's control. Judith Herman, a proponent of this psychiatric direction, remarks in *Trauma and Recovery:* "The most powerful determinant of psychological harm is the character of the traumatic event itself. Individual personality characteristics count for little in the face of overwhelming events."[10] Herman and others have given the traumatic event, not the subject experiencing it, pride of place in contemporary psychology.

The boundary between psychiatric diagnosis and cultural milieu is a blurred one, revealing the delicate inter-relation between medical perceptions and social under-standings. The popularity of these new diagnoses of preference like PTSD and MPD captures more than a change in the characteristics of the clients seeking treat-ment. It also expresses the preoccupation of the mental health community and the national culture with trauma as a central organizing principle to explain various symp-toms. Our current culture is characterized by the diffusion of the category of trauma so that troublesome pasts—extending well beyond war-related experiences and incest—are categorized as traumatic and then turned into narrative through a language of abuse.

"Trauma talk," while originally a response to real-life events of an overwhelming nature, has come to dominate understanding of the self, its past, and the relation of its earlier experiences to present-day unhappiness. Such talk now extends far beyond the circumstances in which this objectivist psychology was pioneered. We have become a society of trauma survivors, as we each describe, think, and feel the past traumatically and understand the present in relation to it. Vietnam war veterans, concentration camp survivors, victims of childhood incest have become the exemplar cases of the past's determination of the present: discursively, we try to understand our own earlier expe-riences, and those of our patients, through these traumatic filters.

Yet, as Hacking reminds us, the link between symptom and cause depends upon a remembering individual engaged in the constitutive work of linking past to present. There is no connection between prior trauma and PTSD or MPD symptoms unless an individual produces the connec-

tion and, by actively seeking his or her own cure, gives
meaning to it. Because of the cultural salience of trauma,
we tend to ignore the subjective process by which an individual relates the past to the present. We leave out of the
curative loop the role of culturally bounded remembering
by individuals attempting to understand the past's relation
to their present unhappiness. In assuming an airtight connection between trauma and dissociation or trauma and
stress disorders and in holding firmly to the conviction that
external experience plays a determinative role in a person's
inner world, we neglect personal subjectivity. Even to the
rememberers, who are participants in this same cultural
universe, cure seems to derive from the return to the
trauma, not from the ways in which the past is remembered.

Thus we live in an age that, though profoundly psychological in its talk about the influence of traumatic pasts on
the present, has created a particularly antipsychological
psychology. It is an age that externalizes the self and, in so
doing, subdues subjectivity. That we both privilege external circumstances as determinative and view memory as a
return to the decisive past prompts Hacking to ask the following questions:

> How come we are stuck with the very earliest, simplest,
> kindergarten Freud, the stock-in-trade of those prewar
> black-and-white psychodramas shown on late-night tele-
> vision? How come we have not even gone so far as Freud
> had gone by 1899—how come we have not thought seri-
> ously about what Freud called screen memories? Why
> have we been so literalist, so mechanical, and imagined
> that an illness produced by trauma is produced at the time
> of the trauma, in early childhood? Why can't we at least
> discuss the idea that the experience of the original event,

apparently kept in memory, is not what causes distress and disfunction; why can't we ask whether the problem comes from the possibly repressed memory itself, much later in life, and the way in which the mind has worked on and recomposed that memory?[11]

Freud-Bashing and the Culture Wars

An indication that our preoccupation with trauma has cultural sources can be seen in the positive public reception of Jeffrey Masson's attack on Freudian psychoanalysis, *The Assault on Truth: Freud's Suppression of the Seduction Theory*, published in 1984. The attention this book received was a cultural analog to the intensifying focus in the early 1980s on the external sources of psychological pain. Masson charges that Freud, when he rejected his own theory that psychoneuroses stemmed from sexual molestation, came to privilege fantasy and the Oedipus complex—figments of the individual's imagination—over the reality of physical, sexual, or emotional abuse of children by adults. Masson argues that as a result Freud and his followers have tended to treat memories as fantasies, or as products of a psychic reality that has little relation to actual trauma. And in treating memories of abuse as neurotic fiction, Masson says, "the analyst, no matter how benevolent otherwise, does violence to the inner life of his patient and is in covert collusion with what made her ill in the first place."[12]

Masson's celebration of the early Freud and broadside against the Freud who turned against his own seduction theory express the contemporary effort to privilege external reality as the source of personal unhappiness, to reject a conception of an autonomous psychic reality, and to make unproblematic the relation between trauma and temporality. Masson's accusations resonated with and supported this antipsychological psychology, which insists on a material correspondence between a given episode in a person's life—call it trauma—and a specific form of illness. This was a line of argument—a form of crude or direct materialism—that Freud aspired to early on but later felt compelled to reject. When Masson says "I think sexual abuse in childhood has a good claim *on being the source* of a good deal of later human suffering, especially for women," he reflects the antisubjectivist spirit of our age.[13] He also reflects a return to many of the cultural presumptions prominent in the 1880s and 1890s from which Freud ultimately extricated himself.

In the same spirit, the more recent work of Bessel A. Van der Kolk and Onno Van der Hart asserts the primacy of trauma for psychological theory. Van der Kolk, a professor at Boston University and a former director of the trauma clinic at Massachusetts General Hospital, and Van der Hart, a professor at Utrecht University in the Netherlands and vice-president of the International Society for the Study of Multiple Personality and Dissociation, have turned their attention to "the role of overwhelming experiences on the development of psychopathology."[14] They challenge Freud's concept of repression—the capacity of an individual to forget for defensive purposes—and suggest that there is no scientific basis for the theory of human subjectivity upon which the concept is based. Repression, they argue, too strongly implies an active impulse to forget; in so doing, repression connotes the subjective choice to forget, not an *automatic* response to overwhelming experience.

In place of Freud, Van der Kolk and Van der Hart seek

to revive interest in Freud's contemporary Pierre Janet, whose interest in trauma and dissociation is more resonant with the psychological commitments and cultural orientation of our era: "For the past seventy-five years, psychoanalysis, the study of repressed wishes and instincts, and descriptive psychiatry virtually ignored the fact that *actual memories* may form the nucleus of psychopathology and continue to exert their influence on current experience by means of the process of dissociation." Whereas Freud moved toward an explanation of psychopathology focusing on conflict-ridden aggressive and sexual impulses that need to be repressed, he moved away from an approach, forged by Janet, recognizing the mental processes that prevent overwhelming experiences from being integrated into consciousness. "While psychoanalysis thereby came to emphasize the force of forbidden wishes, it ignored the continued power of overwhelming terror." The result, as Janet made clear, is not repression, but dissociation: "unassimilated scraps of overwhelming experiences" that remain unintegrated and, as a consequence, out of consciousness.[15]

This model of the mind, according to which overpowering experience generates split or multiple consciousness, has emerged as the dominant model that both challenges a Freudian metapsychology and defines a course of treatment in which traumatic memory must be recovered and integrated within "narrative memory." As Van der Kolk and Van der Hart put it, people "suffer, as Janet said, from a phobia for the traumatic memory." Here, a healthy individual is defined as one whose life experience is integrated into a single consciousness, who has a single narrative language that allows the present to be understood as continuous with the past, and for whom no dimension of past experience is extruded from consciousness, or from the narrative telling of the life story. "In order for this to occur successfully, the traumatized person has to return to the memory often in order to complete it." Memory, it should be noted, is used uncritically here to mean the objective record of past experience, a true record of what happened. Dissociation, when it occurs, interferes with the individual's ability to access the past and to generate a story of the link between prior history and present experience.[16]

The compatibility between this trauma-based theory of memory and Freud's early understanding is telling. The "talking cure," as Freud and Breuer called their new therapeutic method, consisted of discovering the source of the current memory disorder so as to undo psychological repression and relieve the patient from hysterical symptoms. Once memory is retrieved, Freud and Breuer optimistically asserted, symptoms will disappear and cure will result.

Today's understanding of memory as external to symbolic mediation, which coincides with Freud's early assumptions, helps account for the current interest in hypnosis as a therapeutic tool for memory recovery. Hypnosis, like trauma, was a European and American preoccupation in the 1880s and 1890s and has now regained a respected place in psychotherapy. It is viewed as a technique of memory recovery: through hypnotic trance a person may recover events and experiences no longer accessible to conscious recollection.[17] While the focus on trauma reveals a conviction of the determinate role of externally caused experiences, hypnosis celebrates the capacity of the hypnotized person, no longer fettered by conscious inhibition or repression, to return to those determinative events. Through remembering, the person recovers the importance of those events for self-understanding. Hypnosis is now seen as an often effective aid in the enterprise of narrativizing one's life, of developing the ability to tell the complete story of one's past in order to situate it in relation to one's present.

In addition, hypnosis is now seen, as it was a hundred years ago, as a way to re-create dissociative states in a therapeutic setting, where they can be controlled and worked on. As Judith Herman points out, dissociation possesses powerful similarities with hypnotic trance states: "They share the same features of surrender of voluntary action, suspension of initiative and critical judgement, subjective detachment or calm enhanced perception of imagery, altered sensation, including numbness and analgesia, and distortion of reality, including depersonalization, derealization, and change in the sense of time."[18] Through hypnosis, those features of the past that are interfering with healthy functioning in the present can be identified and treated.

Because dissociation implies, in David Spiegel's words, "a kind of divided or parallel access to consciousness," hypnosis has come to be understood as a vehicle of reclamation. Hypnotic trance allows direct and immediate contact with the split-apart consciousness, and offers the hope that its recovery through memory will make possible its integration within a single narrative retelling of the past. Hypnosis now, as in the work of Janet, the American pioneer of hypnosis Morton Prince, and the early Freud, promises the recovery of single consciousness and the end to a dissociated state of being.[19]

Thus in our particular cultural moment what remains of Freud is his earliest psychoanalytic writings, ones that he later substantially modified. Both his critics and his supporters demarcate this early Freud, the "seduction theorist," from a later Freud who replaced a conception of the determinativeness of external reality with a preoccupation with the unconscious, fantasy, and psychic reality. So, for example, the historian John Toews, a "friendly" interpreter of Freud, reminds us that Freud posited the seduction theory only for a short time: within weeks he was reworking it, and he soon abandoned the idea that memories were such straightforward psychological mirrors of objective reality. What was changing, Toews argues, was Freud's understanding of the relation of psychic life to the external world. The seduction theory was premised on an immediate correspondence between thought and reality: in service to this premise, Freud laboriously mined indirect and fragmentary evidence offered by his patients and from it deduced seduction scenes. In general Freud did not hear from his patients explicit stories of incest and sexual abuse; he imagined them. Toews, working within a tradition of scholarship that seeks to explain Freud's original commitment to the seduction theory from the perspective of his later writings, concludes:

> The collapse of the seduction theory in the fall of 1897 was marked by a collapse of Freud's confidence in his ability to use evidence from his patients' fantasies in reconstructing the real history of event sequences . . . but this collapse was transformed into a "triumph" by his recognition that fantasies might be read in a different way,

as signs of the unconscious intentions that produced them rather than of the forgotten events to which they referred. From this perspective the "embellishments" and "sublimations" of fantasy were not so much outworks to be demolished as obscure revelations of a different kind of truth, the truth of unconscious psychical activity. They were openings into a hidden world of "psychic reality" that was not passive and objective but active and subjective, a world of unconscious psychosexual desire.[20]

Other "friendly critics" characterize Freud's early adoption of the seduction theory as a consequence of his failure to distinguish his own theoretical model of mental functioning from that of hypnotic suggestion. Freud was unable to conceptualize the place of the "other" in therapeutic work and to distinguish internally generated fantasies from externally derived expectations; in his early clinical experience he did not sufficiently appreciate the role he himself played in the outcome of the interactions with his patients. Alexander Schusdek, for example, notes that Freud, when working with hysterical patients early in his career, was interested in modifying hypnotic technique to accommodate those who could not be hypnotized. He developed a "pressure technique," asking patients to focus on a symptom while assuring them that something significant would occur to them as he pressed their foreheads. Schusdek tells us that "he expressed great confidence in this procedure and repeated it as often as necessary until the desired material emerged."

One must consider the possibility that the seduction theory was to some degree an artifact of the "pressure technique." The patient was told that something would occur to him when his forehead was pressed. He understood that his recovery was dependent upon it. The procedure was repeated as often as necessary. Associations which were not deemed adequate to explain the symptoms were rejected. The patients may have received some cues from the therapist. In some cases they were warned against the scenes which would emerge. These they reproduced under "the strongest compulsion of the treatment" with uniformity in detail, until the frequency with which fathers were accused of perversions aroused suspicion. Under such circumstances it is difficult to distinguish between the relative contribution made by the patients' memories and phantasies, and the therapists' expectations.[21]

In another provocative article, M. B. MacMillan proposes that Freud's failure, early in his theorizing, to understand transference resulted in the seduction theory. Heavily influenced by physiological models of causation, MacMillan argues, Freud sought the objective event—the trauma—that might produce the psychic result of hysteria. This reasoning was consistent with the scientific models of the day, and Freud vigorously pursued the recovery of memory of sexual trauma. But what Freud did not consider was the possible role of unconscious and indirect suggestion in the eliciting of such memories. "At the beginning of the period in which the theory of childhood seduction was formulated," MacMillan says, "Freud had three specific expectations. They were: first, that sexual factors would prove to be causes of all neuroses; second, that the cause of a given disorder would have to be of a uniform kind; third, that a traumatic memory would be recognizable by the effects of its abreaction."[22]

Without a theory of transference Freud could not understand how his own expectations might shape the memory process of his patients. He was forced to conclude that "if a memory of a childhood seduction was recalled, it followed that a real seduction must have taken place, for in no other way could that memory have appeared at the core of the logical and associative structure." But MacMillan argues that in offering substantiating evidence to support Freud's theory of traumatic causation, his patients, in fact, were demonstrating the powerful role of the transference relationship in memory reconstruction. What were produced, MacMillan suggests, were pseudo-memories, "fabricated during treatment as the patient had come to divine Freud's expectations."[23]

Both his supporters and his detractors see Freud as having been involved in this struggle to abandon the real on behalf of the imagined. Trauma and traumatogenesis, his original preoccupations in accounting for psychopathology, were no longer of concern to him. An interest in psychic realities replaced his interest in traumatic events. From his early emphasis on "the talking cure" as a process of integrating forgotten experience into a narrative life story and self-understanding, Freud moved on to an appreciation of the limits of suggestion in effecting cure. When he abandoned his original view of psychic reality as a mirror of the objective world and as the internal impetus for repression, Freud discovered instinctual drives like sexuality and aggressivity. While his critics insist that Freud's renunciation of the seduction theory was a fundamental misstep, his supporters defend his shift in interest toward the person's inner world. Both friends and foes understand Freud's later psychoanalytic writings as constituting a decisive break with his earliest analytic formulations.

This debate about Freud and his legacy captures the polarized nature of contemporary discourse about the objective and determinative character of the external world versus the subjective and interpretative nature of the inner world, the fixedness of social reality versus its socially constructed character, individual accountability versus societal culpability. Freudian theory has come to occupy a special iconic status in the debate, symbolizing what is at stake in the public discourse: Do we hold the individual responsible for his or her own unhappiness, as Freudian theory—when taken to its extreme—more or less propounds? Or do we endeavor to identify others who have caused the individual's unhappiness by exposing the individual to traumatic experiences? Can clinicians best assist their patients by helping them locate external sources of their unhappiness, and by helping them to integrate these experiences into their consciousness? Or should clinicians rather explore the complex and endogenous mental constructions that may or may not be consequences of traumatic experiences but that nonetheless perpetuate unhappiness?

This tendency to dichotomize Freudian theory echoes the contending cultural positions vying for dominance today, which express modern moral uncertainties at least as much as scientific controversies. I believe the argument about the two Freuds is a result, not the source, of this broader culture war. Freudian theory has come to symbolize the ultimate victory of subjectivity over objectivity, of irrationality over rationality, of endogenous responsibility over exogenous culpability. Because of this, contemporary debates around these themes inevitably draw Freud and psychoanalysis into the discussion.[24] But this understanding of Freud as a great thinker who abandoned his original insights and started anew obscures elements of his encounter with human psychology that remained coherent, though evolving, throughout his career.

In all this controversy, memory is held hostage. Ian Hacking notes that our preoccupation with the problem of memory enables us to participate in a secularized discourse on the soul, and that this profoundly religious concern with the nature and fate of man is what animates our concern with the science of memory.[25] Is memory a form of historical reclamation? Or is remembering a subjective process, affected by interest and desire? Is there conceptual space between memory and history, as the later Freud would argue?

If Hacking is correct, as I believe he is, psychoanalysis has come to serve largely as the scientific foil for this religious discussion, and Freud himself as an anti-Christ. As a result, Freud evokes antipathy in his detractors, who identify in him the source of today's moral crisis, and sympathetic (perhaps apologetic) understanding in his beleaguered defenders. What I propose in place of these polarized positions is an empathic encounter with Freud as he struggled throughout his career with thorny issues—of both scientific and moral import—concerning trauma, memory, and symptom, on the one hand, and the relation of cure to hypnotic suggestion and to personal accountability, on the other.

Freud and Traumatic Memory

In "The Aetiology of Hysteria," one of his earliest psycho-analytic writings, Freud makes this assertion: "Sexual experiences in childhood consisting in stimulation of the genitals, coitus-like acts, and so on, must therefore be recognized, in the last analysis, as being the trauma which leads to hysterical reaction to events at puberty and to the development of hysterical symptoms."[26] Here, in a sentence, is Freud's early, and complex, seduction theory.

First, trauma is created externally. In this case, trauma is the result of the premature manipulation of the genitals, an experience the child is incapable of integrating into his or her own experience. Second, Freud offers a theory of repression—what might be called motivated forgetting—in which, as a result of the overflow of physical sensation, the individual instinctively propels the experience out of consciousness so as to isolate, and thus better tolerate, the surplus feeling generated by the trauma. But when during puberty the genitals are again experienced sexually, repression of the original traumatic event is threatened and efforts to ward off remembering intensify. The consequence is the development of hysterical symptoms: a kind of psychic compensation for forgetting. Freud's seduction theory, then, is premised on external trauma setting into motion internal responses that are intended to protect the individual from the trauma but that produce neurotic symptoms. From this theory Freud and Breuer arrived at their formulation, now fully embraced by many involved in treating trauma, that "hysterics suffer mainly from their reminiscences."

Shortly after propounding his "solution" to neurotic

symptoms, Freud began to rework it, and could not hold on to his momentary sense of accomplishment. But there were elements of this original formulation that Freud never abandoned and upon which he continued to work until the end of his career. In *Moses and Monotheism*, written in 1939, Freud reveals, not a radical disjuncture in his thinking from his earliest psychoanalytic writings, but rather powerful continuities.

Indeed, Freud's project might well be understood as an effort to transcend the categories of distinction that still afflict us, the polarizing ideas of inner and outer, objective and subjective, rational and irrational, when encountering the human psyche. By offering an inclusive model of the mind and of society, Freud hoped to overcome traditional modes of understanding. To be sure, he was not always, or consistently, successful in this effort. But by insisting on dichotomizing Freud, we risk overlooking this achievement: his offering of a way of understanding memory and trauma, narrativity, suggestion, and personal accountability that is an alternative to the all too familiar polarizing and alienative approaches.

Freud struggled throughout his career with two themes that undermined conventional thinking on these issues. First, he considered how the passing of time modifies the nature and character of experience. The place of temporality in human experience and in psychic life had, before Freud, been badly underconceptualized. Second, he explored how traumatic experience, especially if experienced in childhood, is repeated and relived, often unconsciously, during the course of one's life. The repetition compulsion became a cornerstone of Freud's understanding of psychic reality. As he recognized its debilitating effects and its contribution to human suffering, he became less interested in narrative or the "talking cure" as the central route to psychological health. These themes of temporality and repetition have not been at the heart of the discourse about Freud. And yet, without attending to them, we cannot fully grasp Freud's contribution to the overthrow of the traditional modes of thinking.

Temporality

The seduction theory itself carries the first indications that Freud would, in time, make temporality and psychic reality cornerstones of a theory that would explode traditional distinctions between the mind and the outer world, between external events and subjective experience. The seduction theory, after all, included an appreciation of the ability of the mind to remember falsely; this early theory of repression constituted an appreciation of the roles of time and motive in separating the experience of remembering from the event itself. Thus, while the seduction theory is currently presented as a counterfoil to Freud's later writings, its revolutionary elements should not be overlooked. As Richard Wollheim explains it:

> In the first place, it [the seduction theory] insisted that symptoms must be traced back to events that possess "the suitability to serve as a determinant" or are endowed with adequate "traumatic force." Too often, Freud thought, in the explanation of a disorder, events are invoked that are "at once innocuous and unrelated to the character of the hysterical symptom." No one could say this of infantile seductions. Secondly, the theory provided

an answer to the question that was always to puzzle Freud: Why should ideas with a sexual content be found "incompatible" and repressed? Why should not sexuality be simply enjoyed, at any rate to the extent that the maturity of the person permitted? And the answer it gives is in terms of a discrepancy in excitement between the original event, which means little to the infant, and the memory, for which the adolescent is quite unprepared and to which he therefore reacts abnormally or pathologically.[27]

In the consideration of the nature of memory, and in the search for early traumatic events that have the capacity to generate neuroses, the seduction theory was continuous with, not antithetical to, Freud's later work. In the late essay *Moses and Monotheism*, for example, Freud elaborates on themes first introduced in his early theoretical writings:

It may happen that a man who has experienced some frightful accident—a railway collision, for instance—leaves the scene of the event apparently uninjured. In the course of the next few weeks, however, he develops a number of severe psychical and motor symptoms which can only be traced to his shock, the concussion or whatever else it was. He now has a "traumatic neurosis." It is a quite unintelligible—that is to say, a new—fact.[28]

Here Freud posits trauma as synonymous with a latency period, a time in which the experience exists outside conscious understanding or control. It is unintegrated experience. "We give the name of *traumas* to those impressions, experienced early and later forgotten, to which we attach such great importance in the aetiology of the neuroses."

Trauma and the period of latency do not inhere in the originary events; rather, they reveal the differences in capacity of individuals to assimilate and integrate experience into consciousness. Trauma is defined by Freud as this "new fact" created by both an initiating event and the individual's failure to *experience* that event. This is a more subtle and complex rendering of the problem than that in "The Aetiology of Hysteria," because Freud now clearly attributes traumas not to the events themselves but rather to the person's inability to integrate the impulses or sensations that are stimulated by the memory of the events:

> We must often resign ourselves to saying that all we have before us is an unusual, abnormal reaction to experiences and demands which affect everyone, but are worked over and dealt with by other people in another manner which may be called normal. When we have nothing else at our disposal for explaining a neurosis but hereditary and constitutional dispositions, we are naturally tempted to say that it was not acquired but developed.[29]

Freud's idea that neurosis is acquired, rather than a result of a hereditary and constitutional disposition toward its development, shifts the explanation of psychopathology away from the internal programming of the individual and also away from the traumatic event itself. In insisting that neurosis has a temporal dimension, Freud emphasizes the processing over time within the individual, which has the potential to create psychopathology. Traumatic neurosis, like that of the man in the railway accident, expresses a person's incapacity to process the experience "normally."

Freud insists that each individual processes and organizes experience idiosyncratically. At the same time, he asserts that when neuroses occur, they do so in a structured and patterned way, a function of the particularly human character of the illness. Because neuroses possess this logical and associative structure, they are comprehensible to the scientist/clinician, the sufferers can be made aware of the ideational and emotional sources of their illness, and therefore neuroses are treatable diseases. In this respect, Freud never abandoned his central conviction, articulated early in his career, that traumatic reactions, whenever they occur, are associative references to traumatic moments in early childhood.

So, for example, when Freud considers the experience of shell shock among World War I soldiers, he deemphasizes the psychic mechanism of repression and conceptualizes trauma in terms of a process in which the experience remains outside of, or dissociated from, consciousness. The wartime events evoke the prerepresentational experience of maternal trauma, as Ruth Leys has argued; war becomes modeled on the child's earliest reactions to the loss of its mother. Thus Freud increasingly comes to appreciate the role of the passage of time in a person's ability to discover the sources of his or her neurosis. This underscores the centrally interconnected problems with which he struggled throughout his career: the subjectivity of memory, the relation of present symptoms to originary traumatic experience, and the difficulty of enlisting memory on behalf of overcoming neuroses rather than preserving them.[30]

In *Moses and Monotheism* Freud describes the central features of these early traumas: that they occur in early childhood, up to about the fifth year; that they are not accessible to memory, falling as they do within the period of infantile amnesia; and that "they relate to impressions of a sexual and aggressive nature, and no doubt also to early injuries of the ego (narcissistic mortifications)."[31] Early sexual traumas unconsciously frame the meaning and significance of later, potentially traumatic, experience.

While this formulation is from late in Freud's writings, the issue of memory is identified early in his work and persists largely unchanged. In *Project for a Scientific Psychology,* for example, written in 1895, Freud argues that trauma consists of two scenes. The first, occurring in early childhood, has sexual content but no meaning. It is—more or less—pure sensation. But after puberty, trauma typically has no sexual content but is given sexual meaning.[32]

In his 1899 article "Screen Memories" Freud elaborates on this postulate that memory is a joint product of fantasy and reality, recognizing explicitly that "there is in general no guarantee of the data produced by our memory." In the article's imaginary conversation between Freud and a patient who tries to remember, this statement about the unreliability of memory is immediately followed by: "But I am ready to agree with you that the scene is genuine." This is Freud's conundrum. "What Freud came to see," Richard King tells us, "was that 'interest'—the interweaving of desire and defense, put memory in its service; behind all the rigorous probings of memory stood the wish." For Freud, King continues, "*why* we remember and *what* we remember, the motive and the content, are inseparable." In "Screen Memories" Freud powerfully expresses this tangled relation between memory and motive:

Above all, there is the following point. In the majority of significant and in other respects unimpeachable childhood scenes the subject sees himself in the recollection as a child, with the knowledge that this child is himself; he sees this child, however, as an observer from outside the scene would see him . . . Now it is evident that such a picture cannot be an exact repetition of the impression that was originally received. For the subject was then in the middle of the situation and was attending not to himself but to the external world.[33]

In a long footnote to his famous case study of the Rat Man, "Notes upon A Case of Obsessional Neuroses," published in 1909, Freud considers the relation between childhood memory and historical reality. The continuity with his earlier formulation in the *Project for a Scientific Psychology* is evident: "If we do not wish to go astray in our judgement of their historical reality, we must above all bear in mind that people's 'childhood memories' are only consolidated at a later period, usually at the age of puberty; and that this involves a complicated process of remodeling, analogous in every way to the process by which a nation constructs legends about its early history."[34]

Freud increasingly came to focus on the fact that, in Ned Lukacher's words, "in place of the original impression, one has access only to its nonoriginary revision . . . His attention has moved to the manner in which the memory has been constructed through time." Temporal revision, animated by new frames of experience and motives of desire and defense that have postoriginary referents, forever complicates the process of remembering. The genuineness of the scene is of less import to Freud, the analyst, than the ways in which the patient remembers the event through visual imagery—the "scenographic work"—in which the patient imagines himself as the child, as external to himself. The focus on temporal revision, while present in Freud's earliest formulations, does not yet hold the pride of theoretical place that it will later assume. Indeed, when Freud, in his seduction theory, asserts that a memory of seduction reveals an actual seduction, it seems he may have forgotten for a time "the difference between the subject *of* the scene and the subject *in* the scene."[35] Nonetheless, themes of temporality and representation increasingly, from the seduction theory onward, came to dominate Freud's encounter with the process of remembering.

The Repetition Compulsion

These preoccupations corresponded with Freud's self-conscious attempt to extricate himself from a metapsychology implied in the technique of hypnotic suggestion. He struggled to differentiate his method of psychoanalysis from hypnotic suggestion, precisely to distinguish the narrative elements of the therapeutic relationship—the "talking cure"—from the interpersonal ones, which in time he would call the transference. A passage from Freud's *An Autobiographical Study* (1925) captures his battle with hypnotic technique, as he both enthusiastically employed it and later disavowed it:

It related to one of my most acquiescent patients, with whom hypnosis had enabled me to bring about the most marvelous results, and whom I was engaged in relieving of her suffering by tracing back her attacks of pain to their origins. As she woke up on one occasion, she threw her arms around my neck. The unexpected entrance of a servant relieved us from a painful discussion, but from that time onwards there was a tacit understanding between us that hypnotic treatment should be discontinued.[36]

Today's renewed interest in hypnosis, as George Ganaway points out, is accompanied by a lack of interest in transference, either as a source of self-understanding or as a contaminant in the narrativizing process.[37] What Freud accomplished over the course of his career, namely making the relation between the objective and subjective world a problematic one, is largely being undone in today's exaggerated and one-sided claims about the possibility of retrieving objectivity through remembering. By 1896 Freud had fully adopted the method of free association, which he understood as an alternative bearing no resemblance to hypnosis. The "discovery" of free association emerged simultaneously with his recognition of the transference relationship as central to psychoanalytic cure. This link between free association, the transference relationship, and Freud's theory of memory demonstrates how Freud moved from therapeutic technique to metapsychology and back again in generating his own model of the mind and developing his own clinical method.

In an important article, "Remembering, Repeating, and Working-Through," published in 1914 but marking his dramatic shift in therapeutic emphasis over the preceding several years, Freud explicitly distinguishes the psychoanalytic method of free association from hypnotic technique. In hypnosis, he writes, "remembering [takes] a very simple form. The patient put[s] himself back into an earlier situation, which he seemed never to confuse with the present one." But with free association, some remembering assumes the form found in hypnosis, that is, simple remembering, but there is also a second form of remembering, which consists of *repeating* past experience by acting it out. Freud describes "the compulsion to repeat," a theme that would become a hallmark of psychoanalytic theory. This compulsion constitutes a type of unconscious remembering. Remembering of this kind is discovered through the transference relationship:

> We soon perceive that the transference is itself only a piece of repetition, and that the repetition is a transference of the forgotten past not only on to the doctor but also on to all the other aspects of the current situation. We must be prepared to find, therefore, that the patient yields to the compulsion to repeat, which now replaces the impulsion to remember, not only in his personal attitude to his doctor but also in every other activity and relationship which may occupy his life at the time.[38]

Freud now postulates two kinds of remembering. First, he acknowledges, though he is no longer very interested in, the remembering that is easily accessed, where resistance is mild and recollection of the past, as in hypnosis, more easily yields to the narrative form. The second kind is remembering through the compulsion to repeat—experience that resists recall and narration and that can be known only through the transference relationship:

> The main instrument, however, for curbing the patient's compulsion to repeat and for turning it into a motive for remembering lies in the handling of the transference. We render the compulsion harmless, and indeed useful, by

giving it the right to assert itself in a definite field. We admit it into the transference as a playground in which it is allowed to expand in almost complete freedom and in which it is expected to display to us everything in the way of pathogenic instincts that is hidden in the patient's mind.[39]

Yet in identifying this second form of remembering, the repetition compulsion, Freud remained keenly aware that the transference relationship constituted the patient's current repetitive efforts to assimilate painful experiences from the past and that, without suitable intervention, it would simply repeat past failures to master the experiences. In repetition these painful affective states originating in the past are reworked, or retranscribed, in the present. The patient's illness must be re-created, Freud argues, "not as an event in the past, but as a present-day force." "The doctor tries to compel him to fit these emotional impulses into the nexus of the treatment and of his life-history, to submit them to intellectual consideration and to understand them in the light of their psychical value. This struggle between the doctor and the patient, between intellect and instinctual life, between understanding and seeking to act, is played out almost exclusively in the phenomena of transference." "When all is said and done," Freud continues in "The Dynamics of Transference," it is impossible to destroy anyone *in absentia* or *in effigie*."[40]

By rejecting hypnotic suggestion as a therapeutic technique, Freud introduced thoroughly modern conceptions of memory and of time, ones that are now under sustained attack. As Arnold Modell has convincingly argued in *Other Times, Other Realities*, Freud was the first to offer a conception of memory as a retranscription of the past into (often affective) experiences in the present. "Transference repetition," Modell writes, ". . . is a response to the pressure of unassimilated experience."[41] Where simple narrative, that is, remembering, may provide a feeling of coherence and a sense of continuity with the past, the repetitive character of unconscious memory, expressed through the transference, reveals the affective dimension of the remembering process. Trauma cannot be captured or contained narratively; rather, it was Freud's claim, as he distinguished his method from hypnotic suggestion, that trauma is revealed through the affectivity of the transference relationship.

Seen in this way, the contemporary preoccupation with narrative, like the renewed interest in hypnotically induced memory, constitutes a search for historical truth, *as if* that truth can be devoid of affective meaning. But the truth of the past can be discovered, by the person who experienced it, only through witnessing how the past is inscribed affectively in experiences and fantasies and then acted on in engagement with others and with the world. Modell, a psychoanalyst, notes the limitations of the narrative mode: "The fact remains that human lives are not an open narrative whose story lines can be capriciously altered in one direction or another. The analogy between psychoanalysis and the narrative text has been overextended and ultimately cannot be supported because it ignores the fundamental fact that . . . *the past cannot simply be reconstructed arbitrarily because it is rooted in ineradicable affective experiences.*"[42]

Modell is surely right when he suggests that the contemporary preoccupation with narration—both in psychoanalysis and in other therapies—has resulted in a relative lack of interest in affect in the remembering process. The search for what happened, if divorced from the individual's experience of its having happened, leads to a kind of alienative remembering—a narrative account that denies affectivity in general and underemphasizes the therapeutic role of the transference relationship in particular. The use of narrative as a path to self-recovery requires experience capable of being represented through visual imagery and expressed in narrative form—and then reinterpreted affectively. It also postulates a decisive role for repression, the psychic mechanism by which experience is represented visually in one's mind, interpreted for its significance, *and* intentionally (though unconsciously) denied access to consciousness.

Modell's critique rests on his claim that narrative's "one-person" focus denies the fundamental intersubjectiveness of self-remembrance. His criticisms have been supported by psychologists interested in narrative who identify themselves as social constructionists. Their work highlights the importance of others in the construction of a narrative account of a remembering self, and specifies elements of narrative that reveal it as culturally constrained. What appears to be simply an impersonal account of the relation of one's past to one's present, they argue, actually represents a social process through which a self identifies itself interpersonally in a world of others and the past becomes not only organized and detailed but also experienced.

Robyn Fivush has demonstrated that children's structuring of narratives of past events in their lives is developed interactionally, and that the capacity to structure such narratives follows a coherent, identifiable developmental path. For very young children, adults structure both form and content of narratives of the past. As children get older they increasingly produce the content themselves, armed with the structuring elements of the narrative form provided by adults. It is thus both an interpersonal and a cultural achievement when a child masters the culturally specific rules about what kinds of remembered events to include in a narrative account of self-remembrance. Hardly an activity of the isolated mind, Fivush argues, memory is a self-achievement that can only be accomplished socially and intersubjectively.[43]

Similarly, Kenneth Gergen identifies the cultural conventions that operate in the construction of narrative self-remembrances and characterizes the process of remembering itself as a *performative* act. Memory, as Gergen portrays it, is a social skill, achieved in a narrative form, which functions only within a specific social context that provides the rememberer with a cultural code that is both enabling and constraining. Thus Gergen argues that narrative memory, while putatively autobiographical, is a social possession. It cannot be obtained independent of those cultural codes, and experience of the past cannot be divorced from the social meaning it is given.[44]

In this same intersubjective spirit the psychoanalyst Donald Spence, in *Narrative Truth and Historical Truth*, debunks what he describes as the psychoanalytic shibboleth that psychic cure depends upon discovering the historical truth of "what happened." Spence demonstrates the critical role in analytic treatment played by narrative truth, by which he means a narrative of self-remembering that is agreed upon by analyst and patient together. Spence's point is not that truth as such is irrelevant to cure, but that memory is necessarily an intersubjective accomplishment.

The fact that memory is such a potent force in peoples' lives derives from this feature: it carries great affective significance because it is a testimony of intersubjective truths—in the past and in the present—and contributes in large measure to personal feeling and experience. As Gergen puts it: "In the therapeutic setting and beyond, we find *auto*biography as anything but *auto*nomous; it is more properly *socio*biography."[45]

Modell, as a psychoanalyst, shares with these social constructionists a recognition of the intersubjectivity of narrative construction. At the same time, in his reservations about unidimensionally linking the remembering process to narrative he articulates a distinctive psychoanalytic contribution to the theory of memory: an appreciation of the affective, noncognitive, and conflictual dimensions of remembering. Social constructionists, like analysts, emphasize the importance of a mediating, interpreting self, actively participating, in concert with others, in self-understanding. Memory is always *in process*. But Freud, in appreciating the role of the transference, recognized the centrality of the non-narrative dimensions of analytic work.

According to both Modell and Freud, affect is intersubjectively inscribed pre-representationally or pre-imagistically, and thus narrative accounts of the past's impact on the present fall short of discovering the sources of neurotic symptoms. As Mikkel Borch-Jacobsen has argued, transference, for Freud, constitutes the repetition of early object relationships that *preceded* ego or self formation and thus cannot be represented.[46] As in his earlier account of war neuroses, Freud employs a conception of traumatic experience as dissociated and unintegrated with the self or with the ego, preferring it to his earlier model of psychic repression. The remembering of traumatic experiences depends on the individual's capacity to integrate them within his or her own experience, to give them meaning, and to represent them. But this process is necessarily collaborative and forever open-ended.

In time Freud would identify these traumatic childhood memories as "primal scenes," that is, early childhood experiences responsible for infantile neuroses. But in positing these experiences as the sources of later illness, Freud did not abandon his conviction of the clinical impossibility of perfectly reconstructing the patient's primal scene experiences. In his Wolf-Man case study, "From the History of an Infantile Neurosis" (1914), he writes that primal scenes "as a rule [are] not reproduced as recollections, but have to be divined—constructed—gradually and laboriously from an aggregate of indications." "It does not necessarily follow that these previously unconscious recollections are always true," he insists. "They may be; but they are often distorted from the truth, and interspersed with imaginary elements, just like the so-called screen memories which are preserved spontaneously."[47]

While the search for childhood trauma is the *sine qua non* of psychoanalytic work, discovering the primal scene in its completeness is impossible because of the temporal problems involved in remembering. Ned Lukacher puts it this way:

What prevents both Freud and his patient from reaching the closure they seek is the irreducible nature of what Freud in *The Project for a Scientific Psychology* (1895) called *"Bahnung,"* "breaching" or "facilitation," which in the Wolf-Man case he calls "deferred action." No demand for closure, regardless of the personal or collective forces that inform it, can overcome the radical problematization of the origin and the bases of explanation that Freud has put into effect through his notion of the differential pathway, the temporal spacing, that always characterizes the joint work of memory and unconscious phantasy.

Freud's acknowledgment of the constructed character of the primal scene—a scene that can never be known completely and definitively—expresses his understanding of analytic cure as about the *aspiration* for closure, despite its impossibility. In Lukacher's words: "Nothing can halt the process of deferral in which the notion of the origin and the etiology of the event are caught. There will always be the need for yet another supplement, yet another version of the originary function of the nonoriginary. There will always be the need for yet another version of the primal scene."[48]

In recognizing that the recovery of the primal scene is impossible, one necessarily turns to the work of constructing and reconstructing that scene. Here the analyst and the patient are mutually engaged. In a note to the Wolf-Man, Freud says: "I therefore proceed . . . by way of supplement and rectification.—There remains the possibility of taking yet another view of the primal scene underlying the dream."[49]

Analytic work, in short, consists of the collaborative discovery of the ways in which unconscious fantasy and the reworking of the remembered past over time reveal neuroses, precisely because the past itself cannot be known or relived. Analytic work involves representations of the past, not the past itself, presentations of trauma through transference repetition, and understanding of how unconscious fantasy and temporality determine these constructions of self-understanding. But as Ruth Leys notes, Freud's efforts at historical reconstruction of primal scenes assume the centrality of conflict-ridden object relations, and may overlook certain distinctive features of traumatic neuroses.

Suggesting that Freud remained hesitant and contradictory in his efforts to understand, for example, war neuroses, Leys asserts that Freud's insistence that traumatic neuroses originated in anxiety about the loss of the protective mother allowed other analysts, like Ferenczi and later Kardiner, to challenge Freud's formulation. They argued that Freud failed to appreciate the pre-libidinal or pre-object basis of traumatic experience. Following these two writers, Leys proposes that traumatic experience predates object ties but represents a kind of hallucinatory identification with or incorporation of the traumatic situation or person, preventing the individual from emerging independent from the experience: "Traumatic memory is therefore *incarnated memory*. As such it can only be experienced in the mode of a repetition or acting out in the present, not in the mode of conscious recollection."[50]

Trauma and Intersubjectivity

As we have seen, Freud, in two different respects, struggled against alienative conceptions of trauma. First, Freud was committed to the curative role of the analyst in overcoming trauma. Psychoanalysis is collaborative or intersubjective work. The analyst's role in constructing the primal scene, understanding the psychic conflicts it generated, interpreting its contemporary expressions, and aiding the patient to achieve this self-understanding is critical to cure. What can be remembered narratively is not traumatic: however horrible the experience, the individual has been able to incorporate it into consciousness, to integrate it within the self, to represent it, and to experience it affectively. But trauma defies representation and remembering; because it remains set apart from the ego or the self, it expresses itself in repetition. Only jointly with the analyst can the patient proceed toward representation and self-integration. This joint work involves ever more closely approximating the primal scenes—the moments of childhood trauma that cast a shadow over the patient's present life—and interpreting what the transference reveals of the affectively inscribed and unrepresented trauma currently dominating the patient.

Second, Freud combatted the conviction—no less powerful today—that curing trauma requires returning to the past and recovering the traumatic experience. He argued against a view that located trauma in the event itself and not in the individual's processing of it. A conception of trauma as located outside and in the past is alienative. Freud's emphasis on the centrality of the transference struck a blow against such a conception.[51]

After his original formulation of the seduction theory, Freud was no longer in search of the external causes of internal suffering, or of the past trauma corresponding to present symptoms. He came to understand that overwhelming experience generates incomplete remembering. Neurosis is a response not to the event itself but to the faulty process of remembering that succeeded it. And trauma is unassimilated and unrepresented within the individual. Thus, for Freud, the distinction between *actual* neuroses and *psychical* neuroses no longer held its former explanatory power. What required explanation was the variable responses of individuals to experience. In focusing on the internal processing of overwhelming experience, Freud was not rejecting the potency of the external world. Rather, his was a powerfully modern insistence, perhaps echoing back to Hegel, that the distinctions between psychic and external, subjective and objective, even past and present, are, from the perspective of the sensate individual, false ones.

In Cathy Caruth's view, the central Freudian insight concerning trauma is "that the impact of the traumatic event lies precisely in its belatedness, in its refusal to be simply located, in its insistent appearance outside the boundaries of any single place or time." Thus, for example, what is often striking about a memory of a traumatic event is the literalness with which it is remembered, relived, as if no time had passed between the event and the memory of it. The event defies processing, interpretation, revision. It is, as Ruth Leys posits, a kind of hypnotic merger for which there is no self boundary. When the traumatic becomes experienced, that is, assimilated and integrated, it no longer exists as trauma. As Caruth explains:

> This simple definition belies a very peculiar fact: the pathology cannot be defined either by the event itself—which may or may not be catastrophic, and may not traumatize everyone equally—nor . . . in terms of a *distortion* of the event, achieving its haunting power as a result of distorting personal significances attached to it. The pathology consists, rather, solely in the *structure of its experience* or reception: the event is not assimilated or experienced fully at the time, but only belatedly, in its repeated *possession* of the one who experiences it. To be

traumatized is precisely to be possessed by an image or event. And thus the traumatic symptom cannot be interpreted, simply, as a distortion of reality, nor as the lending of unconscious meaning to a reality it wishes to ignore, nor as the repression of what once was wished.[52]

The implications of this perspective on trauma for understanding what occurs in psychotherapeutic cure are dramatic. When traumatic experience is recovered and represented in therapy, the experience is a contemporary one in which what has been external to the self, that is, unassimilated, is integrated into the patient's consciousness. The decisive events in the patient's history come to be represented within the therapeutic setting. But it should be emphasized that the representation reflects the *present* experience of remembering overwhelming past events, not the past events themselves. In representing the experience, the patient is actively engaged in coming to control the remembered events, making himself or herself central to them. Further remembering occurs because of the therapeutic relationship, which promotes representation of experience as it happens.

This is what D. W. Winnicott means by the "delusional transference" staged by the patient. Winnicott writes:

In psycho-analysis as we know it there is no trauma that is outside the individual's omnipotence. Everything eventually comes under ego-control, and thus becomes related to secondary processes. The patient is not helped if the analyst says: "Your mother was not good enough" . . . "your father really seduced you" . . . "your aunt dropped you." Changes come in an analysis when the traumatic factors enter the psycho-analytic material in the patient's own way, and within the patient's omnipotence . . . The analyst is prepared to wait a long time to be in a position to do exactly this kind of work.

These experiences that place the individual once more—this time, omnipotently—at the center of a traumatic moment are now experienced fully from within. For the first time, the overwhelming feelings can be owned, but now in relation to the analyst; the feelings have come under ego-control.[53]

The alienative form of contemporary discourse about trauma, in sum, attacks a richer subjectivity originally offered by Freud. In elevating narrativity in a way that diminishes affectivity, and in privileging past events over present experiences, this discourse underestimates the capacity of individuals, in concert with others, to respond creatively and positively to difficult, even horrible, pasts. It fails to acknowledge the resilience of persons who, with work and effort, can integrate into their present lives traumatic experiences that heretofore have kept them from functioning well in the world. The contemporary discourse about trauma also underestimates the seductiveness of its own claims: in the face of life's difficulties, the language of trauma and narratives of abuse can stand as attractive alternatives to the assumption by the individual, engaged with others, of responsibility for his or her own experience.

5

Toward an Intersubjective Science of Memory

Conventional work in the neurosciences locates the brain as the site where memory occurs, builds on a long tradition of research on brain trauma to discover how the structure and function of the brain contribute to the memory process, and includes fine-grained, inductively based biological, neurochemical, and molecular analyses of brain functioning as it relates to memory. These studies have produced a great deal of new knowledge, about both memory and the brain, and constitute a rich arena of scientific inquiry. The recent resurgence of interest in memory has invigorated neuroscientific research and has led to discoveries about the brain extending well beyond questions of memory. But in identifying the brain as memory's locale, researchers pay most attention to the isolated and isolable properties of the remembering brain.[1]

Because this research looks principally to the structure and function of the brain to understand memory, it reveals the extent to which the premises of science depend on conventional social thinking. In this way the neuroscientific

175

tradition of memory scholarship occupies a place similar to that of traumatology for psychiatry (see Chapter 4). It resists an intersubjective understanding of social life, "objectifies" the brain, and, as it becomes part of commonplace thinking, makes its own contribution to an alienated understanding of the relation between the rememberer and the past being remembered.

By offering evidence to support an intersubjective alternative, I wish to highlight questions and problems involved in understanding memory that typically have not been identified by these researchers. A concept of memory as embodied and embedded yields a critique of the assumptions that underlie much of current neuroscientific research on the brain and memory. Such research offers only a one-sided and therefore distorted explanation of the phenomenon of misremembering, or "false memories." Over the years an intersubjective science has contributed to our knowledge of memory, and I will focus on the postulates that inform this science, but it is clearly only a stepchild of the prevailing tradition of memory studies.

Thus I return to themes introduced earlier concerning situated and site-specific remembering, in order to shed new light on domains of inquiry that have generally been under the purview of the neurosciences. I concentrate on a few subversive texts, drawn from both psychoanalysis and neuroscience, that offer support for the intersubjectiveness of memory. Scholars in the history and philosophy of science have demonstrated that any scientific inquiry is limited by the postulates that structure its formulations. I suggest that the conventional view that memory is an isolable phenomenon, located in the individual, is a product of the assumption that the brain is autonomous both from the body in which it lives and from the social world that it encounters. There now exists a substantial body of research that challenges that assumption, although it has not crystallized into a sustained critique of the prevailing tradition.

Ms. A.'s misremembering cannot be satisfactorily accounted for by conventional science. To describe, for example, her memories of abuse in terms of some form of brain dysfunction is to ignore their context-dependent character. Moreover, conventional understanding hardly generates a satisfactory explanation of the changes over time in the memories Ms. A. produced. Focusing on the truth or falseness of her recollections rather than exploring their meaning in her present life obscures the impossibility of completely knowing the past. We can aspire only to *better* knowing the past; and to achieve that we cannot sequester memory from inner states, motives, or a mediating self.

Memory is one expression of the mind's relation to the body—an interchange between feeling states and mental activity through which an individual strives for a synchronous, harmonious, and continuous self. Memory also expresses the mind's relation to the world of other subjectivities, and to the cultural universe. Understood in this way, memory is part and parcel of the social and temporal coordinates when and where remembering occurs. It is also part and parcel of the developmental process that implicates a person in his or her own past, and that constitutes the person's self in relation to the surrounding social world. In this chapter I return to the embodiment

and embeddedness of memory, with a focus on their implications for the brain. To do so I must enter the citadel of
conventional science on memory.

The Embodied Brain

In his important book *Descartes' Error: Emotion, Reason, and
the Human Brain*, the neuroscientist Antonio Damasio
endorses a blurring of boundaries between what have long
been considered discrete functions of the brain. Damasio
documents the unbreakable link, manifested in the construction of neural circuitry, between the brain and its
body: what he refers to as "the body-minded brain." He
argues that "the mind arises from activity in neural circuits." In this respect, Damasio appears no different from
dominant neuroscientific research that has objectified the
mind as a function of brain activity.[2]

But Damasio diverges from this formulation by insisting
that "many of those circuits were shaped in evolution by
functional requisites of the organism, and that a normal
mind will happen only if those circuits contain basic representations of the organism, and if they continue monitoring the states of the organism in action. In brief, neural
circuits represent the organism continuously, as it is per-
turbed by stimuli from the physical and sociocultural environments, and as it acts on those environments."[3] Damasio
rejects a conception of the brain that either ignores its evolutionary development, a consequence of the organism's
encounter with the demands imposed upon it for survival,
or overlooks the ways in which the brain monitors the
body by responding to representations, or images of the
body, constructed in the brain's neural circuitry.

Damasio makes his point even more emphatically: "I am not saying that the mind is in the body. I am saying that the body contributes more than life support and modulatory effects to the brain. It contributes a *content* that is part and parcel of the workings of the normal mind."[4] To fail to appreciate the connection between the brain and the neurobiological and neuroanatomical adaptations that produce it, as Damasio argues, is to misunderstand both the brain's relation to the somatic milieu of which it is part—that is, its embodiment—and the ways in which that milieu has been shaped by the sociocultural world in which it is embedded.

Descartes' Error challenges our customary ways of thinking about the relation of the mind to both the brain and the body. Insisting on Descartes's contribution to a scientific tradition that demands a distinction between a thinking mind and a nonthinking body, or presumes a disembodied mind and a body uncontaminated by cognition, Damasio argues for a mind that exists squarely within an evolving organism that has adaptively developed the capacity for thought. Thought stands not as disembodied but as the result of an increasingly complex neurological structure in which neuronic circuitry over time developed the ability to mediate between stimulus and response. Rather than existing independently of the body, thought represents the ability of the complex human being to display and order images. These images are constructions from the organism's brain, experiencing the environment (textures, sounds, shapes, colors, space) and mediated through "a complex neural machinery of perception, memory, and reasoning."[5]

Memory, as Damasio explains it, is a distinctive form of

complex thought. It is distinguished from perception and reasoning because its object of attention is a past that no longer exists. But while memory is distinctive in this regard, Damasio identifies it as dependent, like perception and reasoning, on the images conjured up by this unique relation between the brain and the body. In this way, memory, too, articulates the body in the moment as it represents itself imagistically.

Offering a theory of an embodied brain, Damasio challenges any notion that the brain *produces* disembodied thought. It is not the brain in itself that does the thinking—remembering, perceiving, reasoning—but the brain reading the images in the neural circuitry generated by the body. Damasio develops a representational theory of thought, arguing that thinking occurs only through images, or representations, to which the brain responds. From where do these images derive? He explains: "*Images are based directly on those neural representations, and only those, which are organized topographically and which occur in early sensory cortices.* But they are formed either under the control of sensory receptors oriented to the brain's outside (e.g., a retina), or under the control of dispositional representations (dispositions) contained inside the brain, in cortical regions and subcortical nuclei."[6]

Complex thought, in Damasio's view, is an adaptive human achievement, experienced through representations, or images, that express the interaction between the agency of thought—the brain—and the body in which it resides. He argues that abstract thought, or what might be called "meta-reflection," is built upon a substratum of both innate and acquired knowledge, topographically organized and "housed" in the brain and not necessarily accessible to conscious recall. The dispositions toward representation are constructed at a given moment and are under the command of neural patterns—chains or circuits of neurons—elsewhere in the brain, which are typically consequences of lower-order brain activity in early sensory cortices:[7]

> The dispositions related to recallable images were acquired through learning, and thus we can say they constitute a memory. The convergence zones whose dispositional representations can result in images when they fire back to early sensory cortices are located throughout the higher-order association cortices (in occipital, temporal, parietal, and frontal regions), and in basal ganglia and limbic structures . . . Dispositional representations constitute our full repository of knowledge, encompassing both innate knowledge and knowledge acquired by experience.[8]

Damasio emphasizes the *phylogenetic* development of the human being to account for the brain's activity. Brain functioning is a result of the complex historical layering of the brain's anatomy in which higher-order functions are built upon strata of lower-order, more primitive features of brain activity. This phylogenetic perspective finds its complement in the writings of the psychoanalyst Hans Loewald, who emphasizes the centrality of *ontogenetic* development to an understanding of the mature individual. The developed adult, Loewald argues, has acquired the capacity to remember, but memory has not always been a discrete capacity; it is only over time that memory emerges as clearly demarcated from other brain processes like perception.

In his essay "Perspectives on Memory" Loewald emphasizes the acquired character of memories, which develop concurrently with selfhood. In that sense, memory is not an entity but a capacity, a process: "Memorial processes are *activities*, despite the fact that they may, on the one hand, become automatic . . . and, on the other hand, evolve into enduring process patterns that we tend to call structures."[9] In emphasizing memory as present-day activity, Loewald is attentive not only to the ways in which memory occurs in a situated present but also to its close links with the *perceiving* individual. Perception and memory are hardly distinct properties of the brain; they share overlapping characteristics, and in adults the two processes affect each other.

Loewald's description of memory's dependence on perception continues a long-standing tradition in psychoanalytic thought that challenges conventional scientific demarcations of brain functions. Since Freud, psychoanalysis has conceived of perception as an active process, or as Loewald puts it, "not something that happens to a 'perceptual apparatus' and occurs in interaction with its environment." In emphasizing the *activity* of perception, Loewald describes the meaning-making dimensions, or what I have called the embodiment, of an individual's sensory activity, and thereby rejects a conception of perception as isolated from the interpreting mind that perceives. Similarly, he describes memory as a registration or recording by the interpreting agent (the self) in the present and related to a *representation* of the past. Loewald, like Freud, conjoins memory with perception, implicating both in the situated and motivated experience of the individual person in the present, responding to representations of experiences unconsciously registered in the past: "The internal interaction called registration (to be understood in the same active sense as perception) is best viewed, it seems, as a continuation of the perceptual experience, a reproduction in the sense in which a reverberating echo is a reproduction, and not as the resumption of a process that has come to an end."[10]

In *The Ego and the Id* Freud discusses these links between memory and perception. He argues that unconscious "mnemic residues," what we might describe as prior registrations of events and experiences that have been incorporated or internalized by the individual, inform conscious perception of the external world. Here Freud introduces the concept of the "body ego": "A person's own body, and above all its surface, is a place from which both external and internal perceptions may spring . . . The ego is first and foremost a bodily ego; it is not merely a surface entity, but is itself the projection of a surface." In another essay, *Negation*, Freud succinctly collapses the past and the present, perception and memory: "The first and immediate aim, therefore, of reality-testing is, not to *find* an object in real perception that corresponds to the one presented, but to *refind* such an object, to convince oneself that it is still there."[11]

Loewald offers a developmental schema by which to understand why memory *appears* to be distinct from the perceptual processes. He argues that, for the infant, memory as registration or recording is identical to perception. But in time the perceptual schema and the encodings of experience in memory begin to differentiate phenomenologically, to interact, and to inform each other: "The mental 'schemata,' themselves increasingly articulated by perceptual material, increasingly participate in the organization of perceptions, so that percepts more and more acquire structure. Perception . . . is shot through with memory."[12] For Loewald, memory is a set of "crystallized," or "organized," or "structured" perceptions of the past that contribute to the ways in which the person perceives and experiences.

Loewald's psychoanalytic understanding of memory is entirely compatible with Damasio's argument that memory is a form of complex thought organized and structured by lower-order sensory experiences. Loewald similarly insists that memory is not a distinct structural apparatus of the brain but is powerfully engaged with a broad range of human processes by which one's own body is read for its feeling states and through which the world is apprehended and understood. This structuring link between memory and perception helps us understand a particularly interesting feature of memory: that the memories one produces at any given time generally carry a feeling of certainty and objectivity that is only challenged when the same events are remembered differently later on. When memories are revised in this way, both memory and perception can be powerfully reconfigured.

Much research supports both Loewald's and Damasio's claims that what is remembered about the past is influenced by present-day attitudes, emotional and physical states, or what R. M. Dawes calls "biases of retrospection." In a study by G. B. Marcus, respondents were questioned, in 1973 and again in 1982, about their attitudes toward several social issues. In 1982 they were also asked to indicate what their attitudes had been in 1973. The important finding was that their memories of 1973 attitudes were more closely related to their 1982 views than to their actual 1973 views. Similarly, in studies concerned with prior physical or mental states, such as chronic back pain or depression, people's memories of past pain are heavily biased by their current levels of pain.[13]

Contemporary research on hypnosis and memory distortion also lends support to the argument that present-day states of being powerfully influence the memory process. David Spiegel notes that people who are hypnotized typically believe hypnosis increases both the capacity to remember and the accuracy of memories, but that in fact "hypnosis and the enhanced suggestibility associated with it have been linked in the laboratory with increased productivity of memory retrieval at the expense of accuracy, often with a false sense of certainty that the memories produced are correct." Thus, as Daniel Schacter concludes in a review of recent literature on memory distortion, the environment in which memories are retrieved has a significant effect on the memory process, and often generates a conviction of accuracy that empirical study does not support.[14]

Significantly, neither Damasio the body-minded neuroscientist nor Loewald the psychoanalyst limits his understanding of memory to complex, conscious recollection. Each concerns himself with pre-representational experiences—what might be called emotional responses—that occupy an important place in personal life, but that often have neither word nor image to explain them, and that are deeply implicated in the memory process. Damasio, for example, describes pre-representational experiences that express acquired knowledge and are inscribed in the body but not manifested as thinking. He identifies these experiences as "somatic markers," or emotional or affective states that screen out certain thoughts as unthinkable or press other thoughts toward urgent attention: "Emotion is the combination of a *mental evaluative process*, simple or complex, with *dispositional responses to the process*, mostly *toward the body proper*, resulting in an emotional body state, but also *toward the brain itself* (neurotransmitter nuclei in brain stem), resulting in additional mental changes." The body is the site where innate and acquired knowledge is inscribed; it serves as "theatre for the emotions." The brain's effort to "read" emotions, to respond to the sensations they generate, is an effort to reconcile the present body to the memories of the past, that is, to innate and acquired knowledge inscribed in the body.[15]

What is particularly striking, indeed revolutionary, about Damasio's work is his insistence on the body-dependent context of brain functioning. Innate and acquired knowledge is inscribed in the body. The embeddedness of past experiences is written in bodily sensation and feelings, recording layer upon layer of experiences that have been made subjectively meaningful. At times, this pre-representational knowledge—a legacy of past experience—is currently activated or stimulated, demanding recognition by the brain. At times the body as theater demands an audience; the brain is commanded to respond to the script that has been in the process of development since infancy.

Knowledge from the past influences an individual's ability to perceive in the present. And new perceptual experiences sometimes—though far more rarely—alter what we think we know about the past. Memory and the perceptional field are ever shifting over the course of one's life as earlier encodings become reconfigured, or reinterpreted, in light of new perceptual frameworks. This unstable relation between past and present characterizes a uniquely human capacity to carry the past forward into the present while simultaneously reimagining the past.

Damasio does not fill in the content of these pre-representational dramas played out on the body's stage. Psychoanalysis, however, defines itself as being in the business of knowing these primitive emotional dramas that occupy the life of the infant and that continue to inform the experiences of the adult. Loewald elaborates upon this content with particular reference to the question of memory. He argues that memory in the infant probably begins with remembering a state of satisfaction, such as being held or being fed, in "unconscious memorial processes by which the satisfying interaction with environment is continued" during periods when the infant is not being held or fed. The memory of the mother becomes part of the "internal repertoire" that sustains the infant during separations and helps frame perception of the moments when the mother is not available. In Loewald's words: "Memory seems to be inextricably interwoven with experiences of separation, loss, object withdrawal, or cessation of satisfying external interactions. Loss or separation from a love object appears to be a most profound stimulus for the activation of memorial processes . . . Memory is the child of both satisfaction and frustration."[16]

Psychoanalysis conceptualizes the ways in which the external, or object, world becomes internalized in the experience of the individual and is indelibly inscribed in self-image, feeling states, and self-knowing. Internalization of others manifests itself through fantasies of satisfaction and frustration and of pleasurable and unpleasurable feeling states. The internal affective state and the external providers—the first being the "mother-satisfier"—contribute to the process of structuring memory, of distinguishing between an in-the-moment experience and remembered feeling states. Especially important about this process, as Loewald describes it, is that the in-the-moment experiences are framed through prior experiences, structured through memory. Memory, too, as I have noted, is subject to reconfiguration as perceptual experiences work back upon it; in an unending reciprocal process, we reexperience the present and remember the past.

Loewald's analysis is instructive for his characterization of the links among feeling states, memory, and perception and for his understanding of how the three interpenetrate. Memory, he argues, constitutes an organized response to a change in body-feeling, such as a separation from a loved object. And the individual is *actively* engaged in modulating feeling, in responding to disruptions, and in attempting to return to an understandable, tolerable, satisfying, and/or familiar state of being or of feeling. Loewald, in sum, describes an individual with a disposition to find in the environment ways to be that will bring about the end of separation, of loss, of frustration.

This disposition is perhaps a universal one. But psychoanalysis has also provided insight into how some individuals, while seeking a tolerable feeling state, in fact compulsively repeat the mistakes in judgment or perception that prevent them from finding satisfaction. As Arnold Modell has summarized it: "The compulsion to repeat represents a compulsion to seek a perceptual identity between present and past objects." Because these dispositional states are typically neither conscious nor articulate, they are often experienced nonrepresentationally, in body or feeling states of which descriptive words or images, if they are offered at all, can be only approximations. For Loewald, affective states may well result from nonrepresentational remembering, as in the case of anniversary reactions, in which present and past collide and memories of the past shape present-day perceptions. The psychoanalytic relationship allows the discovery of these pre-representational categories through an understanding of the relationship between analyst and patient. As Modell characterizes the transference: "It is a refinding in the present of a category from the past which may or may not prove to be a categorical fit; it is the imposition of an internal template upon what is presented from without."[17]

The understanding of the brain I am offering here emphasizes not its isolation from other elements of the human being but rather its embodiment. The work of Damasio and Loewald reveals important links between psychoanalysis and neuroscience that could advance such an intersubjective science of memory. First, what Loewald captures ontogenetically as the individual's increasing capacity and need for psychic "structuring" in the form of memory, perception, and affects, Damasio explains phylogenetically as humans' increasing capacity for mind's thought: memory, perception, and reasoning. Both note, however, that the mature person's complexity of mental structure should not be understood as evidence of disembodied thought, but instead as evidence of consciousness that is distinguishable both from the brain and from the body, but dependent on and in constant interchange with both.

Rejecting the reductionist impulse to understand mind only in terms of brain, both Damasio and Loewald insist on the human capacity to reflect on one's experience and to evaluate and sometimes alter initial impressions. In emphasizing the consequentiality of experience—both the past as inscribed and the present as perceived—both endorse a materialist conception of human beings in which thought and action are considered to be environmentally dependent and determined. At the same time, both resist a crude materialism that links response to stimulus without mental intervention. Both identify in the individual an ability to reflect self-consciously and to alter memory and perception through thought.

The philosopher Stuart Hampshire, defending a position he calls "freedom of mind," describes this stance that is shared by psychoanalysis and this branch of neuroscience:

> This power of self-conscious reflection upon the mechanisms associated with our first impressions, and the making of thoughtful allowances for our particular standpoint, are as much part of the innate endowment of the species as are the sense-organs themselves. It is natural to evaluate in thought, consciously or unconsciously, the first perceptual impressions that we receive, and the initial beliefs that we form; it is natural to us to move and to change the angle of vision in testing initial beliefs, guided in our thought by the hypotheses that we form about their causes.[18]

Damasio and Loewald understand human beings as developing over time the capacity to reflect upon their own mental processes—even to "correct" them. This plasticity indeed is a hallmark of human beings, because only human beings are able to reconsider, even to reexperience, the past as well as to alter everyday perception in light of their own particular structures of experience. These same properties that describe a person's humanity are what wreak havoc in any effort to establish a "true" or "objective" present or past, independent of subjectivity.

A second link between psychoanalysis and neuroscience is apparent in Damasio's insistence on thought as imagistic and representational. Damasio shares with psychoanalysis a conviction that thinking is necessarily subjective, driven by unconscious fantasies and unarticulated feeling states that only sometimes find their way to consciousness and articulate expression: "Brains can have many intervening steps in the circuits mediating between stimulus and response, and still have no mind, if they do not meet an essential condition: the ability to display images internally and to order those images in a process called thought."[19] Here neuroscience and psychoanalysis converge in rejecting a logic-based, exclusively cognitive conception of thought and reason. Arriving at similar understanding from different directions, both Loewald and Damasio argue that thinking depends on a substratum of images generated by lower-order brain processes and by the body's experience inscribed over time. Therefore, thinking as a mental process cannot be understood independently of the images and representations generated from within.

There is much anecdotal evidence to support the centrality of imagery in thinking—for example in scientists' own descriptions of their creative process as inevitably involving representational thought. This evidence, along with that offered by Damasio, buttresses the psychoanalytic premise of the significance of the unconscious in both thought and action.[20]

A third link appears when, in demonstrating the interconnectedness of brain's activity with body and mind, Damasio describes a powerful mediating *self,* actively engaged in interpreting experience in relation to itself and interpreting itself in relation to the environment in which it is embedded. Here Damasio shares with self psychology an appreciation of the central role of a self that actively aspires to synchrony, harmony, and coherence of experience. This self is ever seeking to order memory, perception, and reason so as to generate an experience of wholeness and singleness, or what Charles Taylor describes as reconciling thought and feeling to an understanding that is "largely inarticulate." The self is always attempting to produce in the world a reality that corresponds with its inarticulate, unformulated, and idiosyncratic relation to the world. Representations or imagistic thinking can only imperfectly capture this pre-objective feeling, but the self acts in ways that conform, sometimes consciously and more often not, to "a sense of what is fitting and right."[21]

Psychoanalytic treatment, seen in this way, seeks to correct the poor fit that occurs when past experiences remain so dominant in a person's present life that they overwhelm the person's ability to distinguish between the lived present and the encoded past. These miscategorizations in which present experience is mistaken for past knowledge manifest themselves affectively or emotionally; they become the communicative vehicle by which the past is brought forward into the present. "Transference repetition," as Modell tells us, "can now be viewed as a special class of perceptual retranscriptions."[22]

In a review of *Descartes' Error,* Daniel Dennett notes that Damasio's appreciation of the unthinking and unreflective decisions that an individual routinely makes while navigating in the world yields a complex and psychologically plausible picture of a self. Dennett suggests that this view of the self in which consciousness is organically constituted results in a "reactivity cascade" that "either satisfies all the 'epistemic hunger' of the active agencies or creates new hungry agencies . . . whose hunger is either satisfied, or not, and so forth." "If all the hunger is satisfied, no alarms ring through the system and life goes on. Otherwise, the cascade continues indefinitely."[23]

In short, individuals actively remember, or perceive, or reason because they are motivated toward harmony, synchrony, or what might be described as a sated or satisfied feeling state, in an environment that sometimes is not so kindly disposed. Memory may be invoked in the interest of reducing uncomfortable, incongruent feeling states: remembering is likely to be a far less urgent activity when "epistemic hunger" is not being felt. Or memory may be mobilized to describe particularly satisfying moments of harmony and synchrony. Either possibility suggests that memory is part and parcel of the plasticity of the human brain, ever adapting to the vagaries of the environment in which it lives.

The Embedded Mind

The Sociability of Remembering

Thus far I have characterized an intersubjective science of memory as presuming the brain's unbreakable link to the body. Recognizing the brain's embodiment significantly alters the kinds of questions asked about the memory process. In my attempt to explain Ms. A.'s misremembering, for example, the concept of the embodied brain provides a way to better understand her misattribution of the cause of her suffering. It is undeniable that she was experiencing overwhelming and painful states of being, stimulated by contemporary experiences that evoked memories of the past, and that the memories she produced were attempts to make these feeling states conscious and more tolerable. But at one stage of the analysis Ms. A. was locating the source of her pain in past events and experiences that probably had not really happened. What remains to be explained concerning her misremembering is: Why was it that *what* she misremembered was paternal incest? Why did those particular images appear in her memory? Why was the painful past represented in the form of sexual abuse by her father?

To answer these questions, I will consider the social character of memory and its relation to Ms. A.'s mind. I will examine the *embeddedness* of her remembering experience, investigating the mind's encounter with the world around it. If the body or inscribed feeling states provide the desire to attribute and to articulate, that is, the motive, the social environment offers particular languages and categories for understanding that provide a vocabulary and grammar of attribution and explanation. The environment presents to the person categories and narratives of experience that have become socially agreed upon as relevant and meaningful to self-constitution.

The embedded mind remembers in culturally particular and meaningful ways, reflecting not only its relation to the past but its involvement in the social world that provides specific access to the past. This content of social experience, the "what" of memory, helps organize an individual's way of being; it contributes to the experience of oneself. There is, in short, reciprocal interaction between body and society: the latter powerfully contributes to what one remembers and how it makes one feel.

A consideration of human emotions illustrates the meaningfulness of the social world for the embedded mind. Emotions invoke a particular personal history; in their expression in the present they conjure up past experiences that contribute to the framing and experiencing of the present. Thus we tend to think of emotional responses as bounded by the body in which they occur, as the property of the individual who is responding affectively. But emotions, like sexuality (discussed in Chapter 3), not only refer to one's own embodied past; they also document one's passionate involvement in the social world. As Stuart Hampshire puts it:

> Under the influence of a passion, we do not think of that passion as a psycho-physical phenomenon issuing from a complication of causes, internal and external. We typically confuse our unexamined love or hatred of someone with a veridical perception of his amiability or hatefulness. We fall into a kind of naive realism in respect of the objects of our attitudes and sentiments, leaving our conceptions of the objects uncorrected by calm and persistent thought about complex causes.

Or, in the words of the cognitive scientist Leslie Brothers, emotions are "essentially interpersonal communicative acts." "Emotions cannot be defined with reference to the mind or body on only one animal or person," says Brothers, rejecting the idea that they are products of an "isolated mind." "If we are to retain the word emotion at all, we should think of it in the context of evolved systems for the mutual regulation of behavior, often involving bodily changes that act as signals."[24]

Our emotional states, in sum, are context-dependent, deeply embedded in the practices and structures of social life, and they reveal the ways in which our body-minded brain depends on understanding or framing experience through a social context. Brothers's book *Friday's Footprint: How Society Shapes the Human Mind* complements Damasio's *Descartes' Error* and helps us make sense of the paradox that emotions depend on an intersubjective world for their expression but are experienced as profoundly solitary. As Damasio documents the historical evolution of the "body-minded brain," Brothers similarly argues that specific portions of the human brain have responded to selection pressure and have generated a cognitive organ specialized for *social* perception. Brothers finds the human brain distinct from the brains of other primates in its capacity to generate from faces and bodies concepts of persons and social order; the human brain, because of its specialized capacity for processing social information, is a "social brain."[25]

Damasio and Brothers allow us to better understand the innate (though social) process by which the individual develops a capacity to discriminate, organize, and symbolize social experience. Understanding the achievement of greater psychological complexity requires understanding this phenomenon of social embeddedness as an acquired phylogenetic adaptation to the demands of species survival and as a natural ontogenetic motivation to "fit in" to the social world. The mother (or other primary caregiver) is the first agent of society: sociality is first manifest in the relation between oneself and one's mother. As Brothers demonstrates, the ability to identify the human face is an inborn one, indicating the human being's adaptation to sociality, and can be observed from the earliest moments after birth.

A growing field of brain research supports the claim that social cognition is a unique feature of the primate brain and is especially developed in the human brain. Particular sets of neurons have been identified as specialized for social perception and behavior. These neural ensembles are located principally in the amygdala and are adaptive to human needs; as Brothers argues, their adaptiveness has corresponded to the human need for ever more elaborate and subtle measures with which to interact and to protect oneself in a social environment. So, for example, a child's visual system becomes especially oriented to faces:

Because of our innate attraction to the sights and sounds of faces, we probably have a considerable circuitry devoted to faces by the end of our first year of life. And all this brain machinery makes us remarkably expert when it comes to faces. For example, we can identify many different faces, even though as a class faces are all quite similar visually. In addition, we readily notice subtle changes in facial expression, as was demonstrated in an experiment in which research subjects were able to detect very tiny differences between similarly comput-erized line drawings depicting facial expressions. We are also extremely acute when it comes to detecting another's gaze direction. Finally, we automatically use information from the sight of mouth movements to understand speech, even without formal instruction in lipreading.[26]

Evidence has accumulated demonstrating the development of a socially constituted self almost from the moment of birth. Leon Eisenberg, for example, in an article in the *American Journal of Psychiatry* entitled "The Social Construction of the Brain," describes brain development as occurring within an "ontogenetic niche," by which he means "in an ecological and social setting that, like its genes, is species-typical for the organism. The ontogenetic niche is a legacy that structures development, a crucial link between parents and offspring, an envelope of life chances." Eisenberg cites research on auditory learning, suggesting that the human infant hears its mother's voice *in utero* and, after birth, is able to distinguish it from other voices. Four-day-old French infants have been shown to suck harder in order to hear French spoken instead of Russian, a preference that must result from *in utero* experience. George Dawson has found the brains of infants of depressed mothers to be organized differently from those of normal mothers.[27]

In 1985 Daniel Stern published *The Interpersonal World of the Infant*, in which he summarized research documenting the development of the self in relation to others almost from the moment of birth.[28] This book has stimulated considerable research supporting the finding of very early self-formation and the development of the self within a social niche. This scholarship does not try to distinguish the brain's contribution to individual development (nature) from the social world's role (nurture): the brain versus the environment. Instead, the critical research question is how the social environment contributes to the structuring and functioning of the brain.

Brothers documents infants' developing capacity to identify with ever finer distinction human faces, gestures, and culturally specific forms of person, and infants' receptiveness to being "instructed" by adults as to their meaning. The infant's motivation to participate in the social world is responded to by adults, who assist the infant as they themselves were assisted in their infancy. In this way, a cultural world of meanings and significances is transmitted from generation to generation.[29]

Brothers locates the aspiration to sociability in the selection process in evolutionary history that distinguishes humans from other species. Yet the specific meanings of these cultural signs are particular to each society and require already-socialized members to interpret for the newborn. Specific cultures are reproduced in the relation established between one generation and the next. Similarly, individuals become culturally specific as they learn, as their brains become able to make these fine-grained distinctions that demarcate them as culturally competent in one particular setting. Brothers describes this process as the learning of "cultural narratives," with language and conversation representing the quintessential sociality of human beings: "The child does not attach utterances to persons because of logical, abstract necessity. Instead, utterances are intrinsically attached to persons because language perception shares the same neural ensembles that encode expressive faces and voices."[30]

Thus the socially competent individual is the socially embedded one, whose self-experience is filtered through preverbal signs and symbols and a language and narrative of experience culturally produced and transmitted by intimate others. Brothers focuses particularly on the brain's adaptability to precognitive structuring provided by the social world, but her work encourages scientific speculation about the ways in which linguistic and narrative forms similarly structure the brain's activity and contribute to the process of remembering.

Remembering Categorically

Categorization, according to the neuroscientist Gerald Edelman, is an automatic function of the brain; in fact, it describes the central activity of the brain. Neurons naturally cluster into specific ensembles, and subsequent experiences typically are processed by being placed along well-worn neuronic pathways. According to Edelman, both lived experiences and concepts are grouped according to their patterns of features.[31] Perception and cognition both depend upon these prior patterns of brain processing and, as a result, cannot be substantively distinguished from the person's already-established and already-coded relation to the social world.

Thus memory is hardly a tangential, or even an independent, feature of the brain's activity, but is integral to both perception and cognition. Yet rather than understanding memory as a mental *property*, Edelman argues that it is a procedure of the brain. He describes memory as a form of recategorization in which the perceptual environment is in dynamic interchange with categorical memory. Without memory as a mechanism to process perceptual inputs according to preexisting experiences, perception would be an overwhelming experience; individuals would not possess the capacity for meaning or organization. Recent studies document the importance of *procedural* memory and establish its presence almost from birth. The researchers Beatrice Beebe, Frank Lachmann, and Joseph Jaffe, for example, have found that an infant, during the first year of life, develops expectations about patterns of interaction with others—particularly caregivers—remembers them, and categorizes them: "These expectations are organized through time, space, affect, and arousal. This is the equipment the baby uses to develop presymbolic representations of characteristic interactions."[32]

The importance of procedural memory, or the centrality of recategorization, in human experience underscores ideas I have already discussed concerning memory's embodiment. New experiences are translated into patterned expectations, associated to earlier experiences already coded into various categories, and, in that way, "contained" or made sensible. New experience, in short, requires an instantaneous "reading" of one's own body so as to organize the new in relation to an ordered past. But Edelman and others acknowledge that new perceptual experiences ensure the dynamism of the categories, producing new, probably more subtle and nuanced frames by which experience is ordered and interpreted. While the categorical foundations may have been laid in early childhood, they are not immutable. New experiences that prove disorienting can generate new categories, new additions to the storehouse of memories. Not all experience finds a satisfactory referent in categories established in early childhood; categorical innovation continues throughout life.

Thus, according to Edelman, what is stored in memory

is not the events of the past in themselves, that is, past experiences, but rather a capacity to refind—in most instances—the category of which a given event is a member. "Recategorical memory is dynamic, transformative, associative, and distributed—its procedures are *representative* of categorizations, but not necessarily representations."[33] In appreciating memory's dynamic capacity, Edelman emphasizes the importance of temporal revision, distinguishing between the present in which remembering occurs—a result of contemporary experience that stimulates the recall of earlier experience now organized categorically—and the past in which experience was coded according to the available categories.

The importance of emphasizing the temporal dimension to memory is to underscore the fact that refinding a category of experience is not identical to representing the earlier experience itself. Earlier experiences are remembered in the way in which they were organized and categorized back then; categorical distinctions of the past, such as time, space, affect, smell, taste, touch, sight, all contributed to the categorization of particular experiences. It is more precise to say that the past is recalled in the present through a particular repertoire of categories developed over the life of the person.

In this way, the present context in which the past is "refound" helps explain the volatility and idiosyncrasy of memory. For example, when a parent and a child recall the same past event, what is remembered and the meaning assigned to it often differ considerably. The two rememberers have clearly recorded the past according to different categories. Similarly, it is well known that the past can be remembered differently as one's experiences in the present change over time.

It is now possible to explain how intense, perhaps overwhelming, experiences in the present can result in categorical errors of remembering. In trying to manage a present-day world characterized by the loss of her mother (which sparked feelings that included both loss and liberation), strong new feelings for her father, and an intense but dangerous-feeling relationship with me, Ms. A. attempted to locate these experiences within her available categorical repertoire. Disorientation and affective feelings of being overwhelmed and in danger of annihilation reminded Ms. A. of a time earlier in her life, a traumatic time, in which she had felt uncontained and terrified of her own annihilation. She was reading her body and attempting to communicate articulately her state of being, both how it felt now and how it echoed her earliest experiences.

While our relationship, in some ways, contributed to the painfulness of Ms. A.'s contemporary experience, it also enabled us to observe how she miscategorized the present because of the restricted repertoire of categories developed in her past. None of the feelings she was experiencing in the present had to be understood as childish feelings of terror and fears of annihilation, and yet by herself she could see no other alternative. Our ability, together, to understand her relationship with me as an expression of a compulsion to repeat her past was perhaps the only way to break the cycle of pain and terror that characterized her life.

But what made the communication, and the transference relationship, even more difficult to interpret was Ms. A.'s attempt to import a new category by which to organize her self-experience. She looked to the social world for a language of pain to account for and to contain the painfulness of her current life experience, and the narrative of sexual abuse and childhood trauma presented itself. She sought to use this narrative to communicate the pain of a traumatic past that was being evoked in her present life. Her pathology was twofold. First, she collapsed present feeling states with past constructions. Memory did not help her constitute herself as a free individual in her contemporary world but rather insisted that she live in the past as if it were the present. Second, she sought to alleviate that pain by appropriating the narrative of trauma and abuse in an attempt to reconcile inner states of being with outer states of understanding.

Self-Expression, Social Understandings

Edelman and the other researchers I have discussed restore to a central place in the study of memory, now buttressed with neuroscientific evidence, the work of Sir Frederic Bartlett, who in 1932 published a monograph entitled *Remembering: A Study in Experimental and Social Psychology.* Bartlett made the argument, novel at the time, that memory depends heavily on the rememberer's preexisting knowledge structures or schemas of past events. Thus he anticipated Edelman's identification of the centrality of categorization in the memory process. In Bartlett's words: "Remembering is not the re-excitation of innumerable fixed, lifeless and fragmentary traces. It is an imaginative reconstruction, or construction, built of the relation of our attitudes towards a whole active mass of organised past reactions or experiences, and to a little outstanding detail which commonly appears in image or in language form."[34]

The particular way in which the past is reconstructed, Bartlett insists, depends on the individual's current attitude toward it. Memory constitutes an individual's best effort to justify his or her particular attitude toward the past:

> Attitude is very largely a matter of feeling, or affect. We say that it is characterised by doubt, hesitation, surprise, astonishment, confidence, dislike, repulsion and so on . . . that when a subject is being asked to remember, very often the first thing that emerges is something of the nature of attitude. The recall is then a construction, made largely on the basis of this attitude, and its general effect is that of a justification of the attitude.[35]

Bartlett appreciates the social influences on both remembering and forgetting—what I call the embeddedness of memory. In discussing the importance of schemas of recollection, he describes the ways in which the past becomes understood and consciously recalled on behalf of the rememberer. But in emphasizing the role of attitude in the appropriation of one schema or another, he notes the importance to the remembering process of preconscious, affective roots.

Building upon Bartlett's insights about the role of the present in the recovery of the past, Ernest Schachtel, in the late 1950s, developed a psychoanalytically informed theory of misremembering and forgetting, processes that, he argues, naturally occur in adulthood. Schachtel suggests that adult experiences of the world, what he calls the "conventionalization" of the world, are incompatible with childhood experience. Amnesia about one's childhood, he argues, results from the development of categories or schemata of experience that because of their largely conventional nature fail to contain early childhood experiences: "The tremendous amount of experience which the small child undergoes does not, therefore, find a proportionate variety of suitable vessels (schemata) for its preservation." He describes the conventionalized schemata of adult life as consequences of repression of less well organized but more powerful childhood emotions. Adult forgetting of childhood experiences results from the taming of the intensity of those affects in response to societal demands for conventionalization, a taming that generates schemata for remembering that fail to contain these childhood experiences.[36] Schachtel, therefore, insists upon the significance of an adult's social embeddedness in shaping the way individual pasts are remembered.

In an article entitled "John Dean's Memory," published in 1981, the cognitive psychologist Ulric Neisser ingeniously explores this question of the significance of schemata for remembering. Neisser compares the tapes of White House conversations during the Watergate scandal with testimony by President Nixon's lawyer John Dean about his recollections of those meetings. Neisser concludes that while both Dean's "semantic" memory (word-for-word recall) and his "episodic" memory (his account of what transpired in any given meeting) were fallible, his "repisodic memory," that is, his memory of the recurrent themes that evoke the events, was largely accurate. Neisser argues that Dean distorted conversations and events because one's memory is filtered through one's own psychology: "Many of the distortions reflected Dean's own self-image; he tended to recall his role as more central than it really was."[37]

Neisser's understanding is that schemata or mental scripts, as Bartlett and Schachtel argued before him, are important in comprehending the memory process, but that individual psychology, too, makes an independent contribution to what is remembered and the significance it is accorded: "[Dean's] ambition reorganized his recollections: even when he tries to tell the truth, he can't help emphasizing his own role in every event." Neisser's appreciation of the ways in which schemata organize memory and self-concerns shape it enables him to join this constructivist tradition:

> I believe that this aspect of Dean's testimony illustrates a very common process. The single clear memories that we recollect so vividly actually stand for something else; they are "screen memories" a little like those Freud discussed long ago. Often their real basis is a set of repeated experiences, a sequence of related events that the single recollection merely typifies or represents . . . what seems to be an episode actually *re*presents a *re*petition . . . [Dean] is not remembering the "gist" of a single episode by itself, but the common characteristics of a whole series of events.[38]

The research I have discussed directs us to appreciate the powerful organizing role of cultural narratives in the shaping and constituting of individual experience. While all these scholars rightly insist that the appropriation of language and narrative depends on individuals' preverbal and precognitive capacities and predilections, linguistic forms also contribute to the constitution of individual selves. Brothers reminds us that the very concept of "person" is a cultural construction, and that while the achievement of the cultural fiction of personhood undoubtedly has precognitive sources, the language of individual autonomy surely plays a critical role in shaping members of the culture to correspond to that construction. It is Brothers's point that the particular self, with its own special relation both to its past and to other selves, arises from the collective understanding and content of "person": "In having selves, individuals are subscribing to the collective notion of a person, which is particular to their culture. The experience of a self is the result of applying a *theory* to account for the organization of experience . . . once we have the concept [of self] our experiences are directly interpreted as manifestations of 'self.' "[39]

This is also the central insight of George Herbert Mead and, within sociology, of the school of symbolic interactionism. The self constitutes itself through its alignment with others and by experiencing itself through the imagined view of the others. In order to develop a self, Mead argues, the individual must become an object to himself. The individual accomplishes this by adopting the attitudes of the members of the group to which he belongs. Erving Goffman, also a symbolic interactionist, underscores the fundamental sociability of the individual self: "In analyzing the self, then, we are drawn from its possessor, from the person who will profit or lose most by it, for he and his body merely provide the peg on which something of collaborative manufacture will be hung for a time . . . The self is a product of all of these arrangements and in all of its parts bears the marks of this genesis."[40]

The school of symbolic interactionism, of which Mead is identified as founder and Goffman as one of the most influential contributors, studiously avoids inquiry into either individual motive or the depth psychology of social attachments. Yet there is ample evidence that cultural narratives of trauma and abuse, for example, have become so powerful because of individuals seeking a language by which to articulate otherwise unbearably painful inner states. This is a unique interplay between cultural tales—which are external to the individual and available for appropriation—and affectively charged precognitive experiences seeking representation and expression. The narrative, although presented to the individual from without, can be altered to fit a remembered past and embraced because of the individual's internal needs. Thus the oversocialized concept of the self, as presented by symbolic interactionists, overlooks the organizing role of inner need and desire and the challenges confronting each person seeking to define inner desire in relation to outer social forms.

This becomes especially clear when we try to account for the current ubiquity of narratives about victimizers and victims. These narratives are not only constitutive of the selves that appropriate them, but are themselves products of communicating selves promoting a particular language—one that iterates their sense of impotence—with which to explain their unhappiness. The cultural narratives of childhood trauma and sexual abuse have, strangely, drawn their particular strength from difficult, unhappy childhoods organized, remembered, and understood in terms of this alienated form of victimizer and victim.

The convergence of psychoanalysis and contemporary neuroscience helps us comprehend the powerful structuring roles that cultural narratives play in self-understanding and self-organization. While essential to these processes, cultural forms are not synonymous with the self. Rather, available cultural resources, such as narrative tales, are appropriated idiosyncratically by individual selves, depending on the individuals' motivation to acquire them. But a concept of the self as internally organized and yet dependent on the external world for self-understanding also helps us comprehend the capacity for misremembering as the individual ever seeks to reconcile inner states and outer forms, present states of being and constructions of the past's contributions to those states. The concept of memory as intersubjective establishes not only the interconnections of mind, self, and society but also the possibility of misreading those interconnections.

Conclusion

In "On the Uses and Disadvantages of History for Life," Friedrich Nietzsche offers a critique of the modern personality. He describes modern individuals as all too willing to subordinate themselves to "History." Nietzsche, writing at the turn of the nineteenth century, captures a contemporary phenomenon, in which personal history—experiences in the past—has come to overshadow, even to dominate, the remembering person:

> History confuses the feelings and sensibilities when these are not strong enough to assess the past by themselves. He who no longer dares to trust himself but involuntarily asks of history "How ought I to feel about this?" finds that his timidity gradually turns him into an actor and that he is playing a role, usually indeed many roles and therefore playing them badly and superficially . . . This is a parable for each one of us. He must organize the chaos within him by thinking back to his real needs. His honesty, the strength and truthfulness of his character, must at some time or other rebel against a state of things in which he only repeats what he has heard, learns what is already known, imitates what already exists; he will then begin to grasp that culture can be something other than

a *decoration of life*, that is to say at bottom no more than dissimulation and disguise; for all adornment conceals that which is adorned.[1]

Nietzsche here takes a stand against history, aligning himself rather with the individual who struggles to resist not only the power of the past but the power of cultural externality. In contemporary language, Nietzsche seeks to liberate the self, mediating between larger social forces and interpreting the world in its own behalf, from the forces that helped produce it. In this same spirit, I have argued throughout this book that the standard understanding of memory (as a recovery of what really happened in the past) has been entangled in a cultural environment that tends to deny the intersubjective, mutually constitutive character of our selves, with our bodies and our social world. As a result, ever more elaborate theories have been developed of the structures and forces that impinge upon the individual person—moving outward from the person's brain and biology (neuroscientific research) to structures of power and control that dominate the individual (social scientific research). This is a stubborn form of objectivism that, in these discoveries of structures and forces outside individual control, asserts the irrelevance of the meaning-making and constitutive features of the subject. Thus in these disciplines individual subjectivity is seriously under-theorized and underconceptualized.

What has been referred to in postmodern social theory as "the death of the subject" has as its counterpart in much of cognitive and neuroscientific studies, including neuro-psychiatry, what might be called "the death of the mind." And reigning theoretical constructs in both the natural and social sciences consider a focus on subjectivity to be a red herring, in which epiphenomenal features of the world are mistaken for the thing itself. Many researchers do not simply overlook subjectivity but strongly argue against it. As a consequence, the identification of external factors that shape, define, and determine the person is as rich and varied as the study of subjectivity is impoverished and neglected. We are living in an age in which individuals have come to understand themselves as dominated by forces from the objective world outside them, forces that are beyond their control. And so it is by appropriating these external categories of understanding that individuals seek relief from painful states of being.

The inordinate pressure on the isolated individual to be self-reliant, autonomous, disengaged from others has led to an eager willingness to believe in objective and impersonal forces that prevent this autonomy. I have called this an alienated conception of the individual because it insists on the separation of the thinking being from the world surrounding it. The conflict between our complex sets of feelings and the imperative to situate ourselves according to external categories of self-understanding leaves us split between internally experienced feeling states and the experience of the outside world.

Contemporary conceptions of memory and empirical research on memory document this powerful cultural impulse to objectify and externalize. Memory studies, as I have argued, currently focus predominantly on the brain, separate from the remembering mind, and on the past, distinct from an interpreting present. In contrast to the dominant understanding of memory, an appreciation of memory as intersubjectively constituted emphasizes memory's embeddedness in the present and its inseparability from the environment—both the social world and one's own body—in which remembering occurs. Let us return to the case of Ms. A. to illustrate the intersubjective way of understanding memory. Now armed with an elaborated conception of the role of temporality from Chapter 4 and a recognition of the interaction of self, body, and environment in memory from Chapter 5, we can posit a more complete intersubjective reading of the memories she produced. We can now see her misremembering as part of her effort to find a "cure" for her pain, and the work we were attempting together in her analysis as one of remembering the past in a way compatible with her desire to transform a painful present into a more satisfying future.

What she was "remembering," in fact, was her feeling—which earlier had existed only as inchoate thoughts and bodily sensations—that she had suffered traumatically. Her presentation of this belief to me in the form of a narrative of past abuse was driven by feelings of unhappiness for which she had had no words or images, and by a socially encouraged process of memory recovery—psychoanalysis—through which she hoped to alleviate that unhappiness. Not surprisingly, Ms. A. was scanning her past for something traumatic that had happened *to* her and that might explain her present pain. She was prepared to see herself as a victim of the past. As we examine this phenomenon, it is important to note that her psychoanalytic work was an *activity* of remembering.

Her relationships to me, to members of her family at the time of the analysis, and to her own bodily feeling states are no less important for an understanding of her memories than is the past itself. By demonstrating that remembering is an active, interpretive process of a conscious mind situated in the world, I have been insisting upon its inter-subjective character. Memory is best understood as after-the-fact representations of the past, reworked as they are made meaningful for the present. Memories may be the result of many retranscriptions over time, but at any given time the rememberer typically experiences them as unproblematic structures or as facts, and as external to the rememberer. But despite seeming "objective," memory nonetheless is stimulated by current needs, desires, and defenses and organized by available schemata of understanding.

We might thus speak rather of the "virtuality" of memory, implying that it is identical neither to the past being remembered nor to the person who is remembering. But if we see memory as representation and not as fact, the memory and the self who remembers cannot be easily disentangled. Rememberers invoke the past to situate themselves in the present and to reconcile a feeling, sensate self with an objective reality larger than themselves. The collaborative work undertaken in psychoanalysis tackles the difficult, perhaps impossible, task of disengaging contemporary motives for remembering from the past experiences that make the lived present less vivid, less pleasurable, and less distinct than it might otherwise be.

Once we understand memory as a post-hoc *representation* of the past and not a *return* to the past itself, we can better appreciate the dangers of a literalist conception of memory that does not consider the contributions of time and the current interests of the interpreter to the remembering of the past. The philosopher Charles Taylor makes this point in describing the "dialogue" between self and other that provides the background understanding that enables a person to act in the world. When a person is unable to construct a meaningful understanding of his or her place in the world, the result is various forms of retreat and an inability to participate fully. To achieve this background feeling of the fittingness and rightness in the world, the person produces imagistic or linguistic representations—including representations of the past. The person creates categories and narratives of the past so as to experience the world's meaningfulness, predictability, coherence, and responsiveness.

Yet if the self, as Taylor argues, negotiates with an external world to acquire categories and narratives intended to reconcile its place in the world, we should not think that the physical body is excluded from the self's engagement with externality. The body, rather, provides the self with what might be described as its most intimate encounter with external reality. The symbolizing self not only encounters a public world of others that, when interpreted through available cultural forms of expression, acts back upon the self. The self also "reads" the private world of its own feeling states, a body that becomes symbolized by the self and acts back upon it. Taylor makes this explicit when he describes the "embodied" self: "Our body is not just the executant of the goals we frame, not just the locus of causal factors shaping our representations. Our understanding itself is embodied. That is, our bodily know-how, and the way we act and move, can encode components of our understanding of self and world."[2]

This feeling state, as Thomas Csordas has argued, is "pre-objective," without objectification through language and other forms of articulate expression, but, especially at times when the body feels discordant with its own self or with the external world, there is an impulse for self-expression, that is, for its objectification in communication.[3] The self, as Taylor describes it, is simultaneously a socially embedded agent engaged interpretively in the world of others and an embodied one, interpreting the physical body and representing it through, for example, self-presentation. This view counters the cultural myth of the isolated mind (or what Taylor characterizes as "monological consciousness"); Taylor's formulation, like mine, requires an appreciation of both memory's embeddedness and its embodiment.

Beyond the ways in which memory is actively involved in the embodying and embedding of the self, we might consider another important feature of Ms. A.'s misremembering: the urgency with which she looked to me for corroboration and understanding of the significance of her belief that as a child she had been a victim of incest. The depth of our relationship allowed her to "use" me to test out alternative self-understandings, or possible memories, at least one of which was too terrifying to try out alone. This was the real advantage of the psychoanalytic relationship: the possibility it afforded to explore the unthinkable.

Perhaps the intensity of her desire for my corroboration of these memories constituted a wish to silence judgment, to quell her own voice of skepticism about the accuracy of the images that were being coherently represented for the first time. Or perhaps she looked to me for support for a self-narrative whose consequences, had she internalized its significance, would have been profound. But whatever the motive, our relationship provided the setting in which Ms. A. could indulge her long-held disposition to redo her self, to discover an alternative self-understanding that would yield less current pain and a better feeling of right-ness or fit.

The way Ms. A. used me reveals how memory serves in the constitution of a self. Her memory was a critical step in a dialectical dance through which she hoped to make herself a vivid and distinct being while finding a way to experience connectedness with me and, through that con-nectedness, to feel part of the world around her. This is an example of memory's embeddedness. It illustrates the ways in which the past is remembered socially, both interper-sonally and culturally.

For a time, remembering herself as a member of the cul-tural category "adult survivors of childhood incest" seemed to Ms. A. to be a solution to this conundrum. My role in her analysis reveals the extent to which the inscribing of a self is *learned* from the other, from the world outside. Psy-choanalysis was Ms. A.'s effort to unlearn one self and to forge another, more satisfying one. What she was learning, through a process of trial and error, was conceptual or nar-rative frames that she came to consider relevant to under-standing the relation of her past to her present.

Memory is part of this lifelong work of selfhood, of orga-nizing and locating oneself in relation to one's own feeling state and also in relation to the language provided by the cultural universe around one. Seen in this way, memory cannot exist without input from the world outside. Remembering is achieved not monologically but dialogi-cally. The rememberer looks to the outside world's frames of memory and experience to understand his or her own relation to an always open, interpretable past. And here, echoing Freud's early statement that hysterics suffer from their reminiscences, my work with Ms. A. comprised finding a comprehensible fit, conceptually or narratively framed, between present experience and the past's contribution to it.

Ms. A.'s narrative of victimization, had she continued to believe in it, rather than enabling her to process and assimilate the past, probably would have ossified its particular version of the past. She ran the risk of becoming a permanent victim, defining her identity in terms of supposed childhood experiences she believed to be decisive in the present. Her past would have been forever sequestered, incapable of being processed in the present. The present would have been victim to the past. She would have avoided a conception of herself as party to her unhappiness, perhaps replacing it with an overwhelming sense of herself as victim.

And because of this significance of her activity, she looked to me for direction and support. I stood as an affectively charged "cultural carrier"; my ambivalent response to the memories she produced weighed heavily upon her as she sorted through contending cultural frames of meaning. Ms. A.'s eventual retreat from this view of herself as a victim demonstrates two features of memory I have been emphasizing: memory as *activity in the present* influenced by one's feeling states and by the social world; and memory as learned *through available schemata of understanding* that meaningfully link past with present and thus provide a sense of membership in the larger cultural universe.

The concepts of memory's embodiment and social embeddedness provide an intersubjective alternative to conventional understanding of memory. In this rendering, memory is activity, actively symbolizing the self's relation to its own body and to its social world. This view of memory challenges the conventional view of the self as standing alone, isolated or disengaged from both the body and society. Conceiving memory as intersubjective restores both the body and the social world to the prominent place they deserve in our understanding of how a particular self is constituted and experienced.

Notes

Introduction

1. In emphasizing the narrative, or storytelling, aspects of psychoanalytic treatment, I am not suggesting that narration is necessarily fictive or a figment of one's imagination. Rather, I take as an essential feature of an action, experience, event, or happening the need to describe it. There are a plethora of alternative descriptions available to describe the same experience. It is a psychoanalytic axiom that there are some narrative accounts that more accurately, or completely, capture an individual's experience of events than others. The psychoanalytic process is an effort to arrive at as close a fit as possible between experience and its telling. See, e.g., Roy Schafer, *Retelling a Life: Narration and Dialogue in Psychoanalysis* (New York: Basic Books, 1992), xiv.

2. Jacob Arlow, "Fantasy, Memory, and Reality Testing," *Psychoanalytic Quarterly* 38 (1969): 32.

3. Ibid., 49.

4. Sanford Abend, "Unconscious Fantasy and Theories of Cure," *Journal of the American Psychoanalytic Association* 27 (1979): 589. See Steven H. Goldberg, "Patients' Theories of Pathogenesis," *Psychoanalytic Quarterly* 60 (1991): 245–275; Jacob Arlow, "The Relation of Theories of Pathogenesis to Psychoanalytic Therapy," in *Psychoanalysis: The Science of Mental Conflict: Essays in Honor of Charles Brenner,* ed. A. D. Richards and M. S. Willick (Hillsdale, N.J.: Analytic Press, 1986), 49–64.

1. Ms. A. and the Problem of Misremembering

1. The case of Ms. A. is based upon real case material, but it has been substantially disguised to protect confidentiality. While I have preserved those aspects of the treatment that are central to my analysis and that illustrate the psychodynamics of memory and memory distortion, I have both added and excluded details to ensure Ms. A.'s anonymity, including personal history and dream sequences drawn from my clinical experience with other patients and from other previously published case material that describes similar examples of memory shifts in the course of analysis, particularly around the issues of childhood sexual abuse.

2. Loewald distinguished between "enactive memory" and "representational memory." The former involves a kind of unconscious, identificatory reproduction of past experience, unmediated by conscious processing of past experience in light of present understanding: "From the point of view of representational memory, which is our ordinary yardstick, we would say that the patient, instead of *having* a past, *is* his past; he does not distinguish himself as rememberer from the content of his memory." "Perspectives on Memory," in Loewald, *Papers on Psychoanalysis* (New Haven: Yale University Press, 1980), 164–165.

3. Ellen Bass and Laura Davis, *The Courage to Heal: A Guide for Women Survivors of Child Sexual Abuse*, rev. ed. (New York: Harper Perennial, 1992), 115.

4. Ibid., 119.

5. On clinical intersubjectivity see Joseph Natterson, *Beyond Countertransference: The Therapist's Subjectivity in the Therapeutic Process* (Northvale, N.J.: Jason Aronson, 1991). Natterson emphasizes the mutuality of the analytic encounter, which produces a unique dyadic relationship as well as a unique process of "self-reclamation" for the patient. Psychoanalysis, one might say, is a practice by which an individual struggles to overcome omissions and distortions of the past in the experience of the present. As Habermas argues, psychoanalysis is a method intended to rid

neurotics of "self-deception," a process in which an inaccessible past that has generated self-alienation in the form of symptom formation becomes known, reflected on rather than acted on, and thereby overcome. The "knowing" occurs through unconscious and conscious communication between analyst and patient, and is made known to the latter by the interpretative work of the former. Self-alienation, in short, manifests itself objectively through external relationships; the analyst is in a unique position, *because of his or her professionally developed capacity for self-reflection* and relatively disinterested social position vis-à-vis the patient, to make apparent to the patient this process of alienation. The critical point is that the psychoanalytic process, in overcoming motivated self-estrangement, requires the encounter between two subjectively constituted *selves,* one with a greater ability to suspend personal interest on behalf of the other. See Jurgen Habermas, "Self-Reflection as Science: *Freud's Psychoanalytic Critique of Meaning,"* in Habermas, *Knowledge and Human Interests* (Boston: Beacon Press, 1971), 214–245.

6. Morton Reiser, *Memory in Mind and Brain: What Dream Imagery Reveals* (New Haven: Yale University Press, 1993), 56.

7. Ibid., 59.

2. Memory's Contexts

1. On recent memory scholarship see Daniel L. Schacter, *Search for Memory: The Brain, the Mind, and the Past* (New York: Basic Books, 1996). For a sampling of contemporary research by neuroscientists, psychologists, and social scientists see *Memory Distortion: How Minds, Brains, and Societies Reconstruct the Past,* ed. Daniel L. Schacter (Cambridge, Mass.: Harvard University Press, 1995).

2. Leonard Shengold, *Soul Murder: The Effects of Childhood Abuse and Deprivation* (New Haven: Yale University Press, 1989).

3. Leonard Shengold, "A Variety of Narcissistic Pathology Stemming from Parental Weakness," *Psychoanalytic Quarterly* 60 (1991): 89.

4. Richard Ofshe and Ethan Watters, in *Making Monsters: False Memories, Psychotherapy, and Sexual Hysteria* (New York: Scribner, 1994), describe the case of Paul Ingraham, a father accused by his two grown daughters of child abuse, who in time confessed to the crimes, though he had no recollection of sexually molesting his children. He is currently serving a twenty-seven-year prison sentence. When asked why he confessed without any memories of these rapes, he stated: "Well, number one, my girls know me. They wouldn't lie about something like this . . . My kids don't lie. They tell the truth, and that is what I'm trying to do" (167). Only after being in prison and away from the army of individuals—from detectives to priests to friends—explaining to him how it might be possible to commit heinous crimes without remembering them did Paul Ingraham retract his confession and develop a belief in his own innocence. Ofshe and Watters describe the powerful interpersonal and social forces that led to his confession. But as Shengold suggests, certain personality features were probably also necessary to effect this outcome. Like Ms. A.'s father, Paul Ingraham was an active member of a charismatic religious movement and held a vivid and concrete belief in the power of Satan to force one to do wicked things. See also Laurence Wright, *Remembering Satan* (New York: Knopf, 1994).

5. David L. Raphling, "A Patient Who Was Not Sexually Abused," *Journal of the American Psychoanalytic Association* 42 (1994): 65.

6. Ibid., 74.

7. Judith Herman, *Trauma and Recovery* (New York: Basic Books, 1992), 14.

8. See, e.g., Simon's articles "Incest—See under Oedipus Complex: The History of an Error in Psychoanalysis," *Journal of the American Psychoanalytic Association* 40 (1992): 955–988; and "Incest and Psychoanalysis: Ready to Acknowledge, Bear, Understand?" *Journal of the American Psychoanalytic Association* 42 (1994): 1261–82.

9. There is anecdotal evidence to suggest that "real life" has

never been as absent in the analytic treatment room as the literature might indicate. Nonetheless, on the evidence of the written word, psychoanalysts' reputation for underemphasizing the effects of traumatic events on the psyche is well deserved. This neglect is being addressed by analytically trained researchers, who bring to trauma studies a psychoanalytic perspective insufficiently attended to by traumatologists. See, e.g., Melvin Lansky and C. R. Bley, *Posttraumatic Nightmares: Psychodynamic Explorations* (Hillsdale, N.J.: Analytic Press, 1995). Also see Robert Pynoos et al., "Life Threat and Posttraumatic Stress in School-age Children," *Archives of General Psychiatry* 44 (1987): 1057–63; Robert Pynoos and Kathleen Nader, "Children's Memory and Proximity to Violence," *Journal of the American Academy of Child and Adolescent Psychiatry* 28 (1989): 236–241; Robert Pynoos, Alan Steinberg, and Lisa Aronson, "Traumatic Experiences: The Early Organization of Memory in School-Age Children and Adolescents," in *Trauma and Memory: Clinical and Legal Controversies,* ed. Applebaum, Vyehara, and Ellis (New York: Oxford University Press, 1997), 272–289; Jacob Lindy, *Vietnam: A Casebook* (New York: Brunner/Mazel, 1988).

10. George Herbert Mead, "Time," in Mead, *On Social Psychology,* rev. ed., ed. Anselm Strauss (Chicago: University of Chicago Press, 1964), 328–341; Maurice Halbwachs, "The Social Frameworks of Memory" in Halbwachs, *On Collective Memory,* ed. and trans. Lewis Coser (Chicago: University of Chicago Press, 1992), 38.

11. See, e.g., Barry Schwartz, "The Social Context of Commemoration: A Study in Collective Memory," *Social Forces* 61 (1982): 374–397; Howard Schuman and Jacqueline Scott, "Generations and Collective Memory," *American Sociological Review* 54 (1989): 359–381; Michael Schudson, "The Present in the Past versus the Past in the Present," *Communication* 11 (1989): 105–113; Barry Schwartz, Yael Zerubavel, and Dernice Barnett, "The Recovery of Masada: A Study in Collective Memory," *Sociological Quarterly* 27 (1986): 147–164; David Middleton and Derek Edwards, eds., *Collective Remembering* (Newbury Park: Sage, 1990).

12. Diana Russell, *The Secret Trauma: Incest in the Lives of Girls and Women* (New York: Basic Books, 1986).

13. U.S. Advisory Board on Child Abuse and Neglect, "A Nation's Shame: Fatal Child Abuse and Neglect in the United States, Executive Summary," Department of Health and Human Services, Administration for Children and Families, April 1995.

14. Paul and Shirley Eberle, *The Abuse of Innocence: The McMartin Preschool Trial* (Buffalo: Prometheus Books, 1993). A Public Broadcasting Production, *Frontline*, carried a four-hour report on July 20 and 21, 1993, entitled "Innocence Lost: The Verdict." This was a follow-up of a *Frontline* report done some three years earlier, on one of "the largest child sexual abuse cases" in the country, in Edentown, North Carolina. Two of those accused of abuse were sentenced to life in prison, though the report clearly presented the case that this was an example of widespread hysteria, of suspect accusations made by very young children to therapists who improperly interrogated them, and no corroborating evidence to support the charges. Similarly, National Public Radio, on December 17, 1994, reported on the town of Jordan, Minnesota, in which, in 1984, 26 adults were indicted for sexually abusing children. The report noted that "prosecutors and police, acting they believed to protect victimized youngsters, took children from out of their seats at school to be questioned while their parents were called out from work to be arrested." Unlike Edentown, in Jordan there were no convictions; instead, in 1988, the prosecutor in charge of the indictments was reprimanded for misconduct by the Minnesota Supreme Court.

15. See, e.g., Jeffrey Victor, *Satanic Panic: The Creation of a Contemporary Legend* (Chicago: Open Court, 1993). The FBI has been unable to document satanic ritual abuse. See Kenneth Lanning, "Satanic, Occult, Ritualistic Crime: A Law Enforcement Perspective," *Police Chief,* Oct. 1989, 62–83. See also Robert D. Hicks, *In Pursuit of Satan, the Police, and the Occult* (Buffalo, N.Y.: Prometheus Books, 1991). A special issue of the *Journal of Psychology and The-*

ology 20 (1992) is entitled "Satanic Ritual Abuse: The Current State of Knowledge."

16. Marina Warner, "Little Angels, Little Monsters," in Warner, *Six Myths of Our Time* (New York: Vintage, 1995), 47. Carol Tavris, "When a Child's Kiss Is a Crime," *Los Angeles Times,* Sept. 30, 1996, B5.

17. Ellen Bass and Laura Davis, *The Courage to Heal: A Guide for Women Survivors of Child Sexual Abuse,* rev. ed. (New York: Harper Perennial, 1992), 22. For other books in the same genre, see Renee Frederickson, *Repressed Memories: A Journey to Recovery from Sexual Abuse* (New York: Simon and Schuster, 1992); E. Sue Blume, *Secret Survivors: Uncovering Incest and Its Aftereffects in Women* (New York: Wiley, 1990); Patricia Love, *The Emotional Incest Syndrome: What to Do When a Parent's Love Rules Your Life* (New York: Bantam, 1990).

18. Carol Tavris, "Beware the Incest-Survivor Machine," *New York Times Book Review,* Jan. 3, 1993, 1.

19. Mark Pendergrast, *Victims of Memory: Sex Abuse Accusations and Shattered Lives,* 2d ed. (Hinesburg, Vt.: Upper Access Books, 1996). AMA cited in the *FMS Foundation Newsletter* 4, no. 3, March 1, 1995, 1. Kenneth S. Pope, "Memory, Abuse, and Science: Questioning Claims about the False Memory Syndrome Epidemic," *American Psychologist* 51 (Sept. 1996): 957–974.

20. See, e.g., Frederick Crews et al., *The Memory Wars: Freud's Legacy in Dispute* (New York: New York Review of Books, 1995).

21. Lawrence Wright, *Remembering Satan* (New York: Knopf, 1994).

22. Goffman captures what I believe accounts for the appeal to Ms. A. of identifying herself as an abuse survivor: "Mortification or curtailment of the self is very likely to involve acute psychological stress for the individual, but for an individual sick with his world or guilt-ridden in it mortification may bring psychological relief." Erving Goffman, *Asylums: Essays on the Social Situation of Mental Patients and Other Inmates* (Garden City, N.Y.: Doubleday Anchor, 1961), 48.

23. Henri Bergson, *Matter and Memory*, trans. Nancy Paul and W. Scott Palmer (New York: Macmillan, 1950 [1911]), xvi.

24. Charles Taylor, "Transcendental Arguments," in Taylor, *Philosophical Arguments* (Cambridge, Mass.: Harvard University Press, 1995), 26.

25. Charles Taylor, "To Follow a Rule," ibid., 174.

26. Lenore Terr, *Unchained Memories: True Stories of Traumatic Memories, Lost and Found* (New York: Basic Books, 1994), 4.

27. See Richard Ofshe and Ethan Watters, *Making Monsters: False Memories, Psychotherapy, and Sexual Hysteria* (New York: Scribner, 1994); Elizabeth Loftus and Katherine Ketcham, *The Myth of Repressed Memory: False Memories and Allegations of Sexual Abuse* (New York: Scribner, 1994); Crews et al., *Memory Wars*.

28. Lenore Terr insists that when the memories emerged Eileen was not aware of the ideas of repressed memory and childhood trauma. But Ofshe and Watters assert that Eileen's earlier therapies, before she saw Terr, had "educated" her about repressed memories and the possible benefits of recovering them. See Ofshe and Watters, *Making Monsters*, 255. It is also true that Lipsker's "cascade of memories" produced ever more horrible incidents of abuse and elaborated details of victimization. Perhaps Terr might argue that this is the natural course of recovering memories: that the most extreme forms of abuse are more powerfully repressed and require more time and effort to uncover. Or, as the critics might argue, the patient may feel a license to confabulate in collusion with a therapist who is looking for more extreme expressions of abuse. This tendency to elaborate and uncover more memories of abuse may express a greater confidence in the "new self" that is being created as a result of the memories.

29. Loftus and Ketcham, *Myth of Repressed Memory*, 97–99.

30. This story of the sequel was reported not in Loftus's book but in her presentation at a conference on memory distortion sponsored by the Harvard Center for the Study of Mind, Brain, and Behavior, held at the American Academy of Arts and Sci-

ences in Cambridge, Mass., May 6–8, 1994. For another description see Pendergrast, *Victims of Memory*, 98–99.

31. I derive these ideas of the "structuring of the self" largely from Heinz Kohut, "Does Psychoanalysis Need a Psychology of the Self?" in Kohut, *The Restoration of the Self* (New York: International Universities Press, 1977), 63–139. For a discussion on the "needs of the self" see Paul Ricoeur, "The Self in Psychoanalysis and in Phenomenological Philosophy," *Psychoanalytic Inquiry* 6 (1986): 437–445. Ricoeur summarizes Kohut's definition of self needs as those "for cohesion, for firmness, for harmony."

32. Oliver Sacks, *The Man Who Mistook His Wife for a Hat and Other Clinical Tales* (New York: Summit, 1985), 34.

33. Israel Rosenfield, *The Strange, Familiar and Forgotten: An Anatomy of Consciousness* (New York: Vintage, 1993), 3.

3. Memory, Culture, and the Self

1. Robert Stolorow and George Atwood, *Contexts of Being: The Intersubjective Foundations of Psychological Life* (Hillsdale, N.J.: Analytic Press, 1992), 7.

2. See Elizabeth Loftus, Julie Feldman, and Richard Dashiell, "The Reality of Illusory Memories," in *Memory Distortion: How Minds, Brains, and Societies Reconstruct the Past,* ed. Daniel L. Schacter (Cambridge, Mass.: Harvard University Press, 1995), 47–68. Also see Matthew Hugh Erdelyi, "Repression, Reconstruction and Defense: History and Integration of the Psychoanalytic and Experimental Frameworks," in *Repression and Dissociation,* ed. Jerome L. Singer (Chicago: University of Chicago Press, 1990), 1–31; J. David, "Repression and the Inaccessibility of Emotional Memories," ibid., 387–403; David Spiegel, ed., *Dissociation: Culture, Mind and Body* (Washington: American Psychiatric Press, 1994); D. S. Lindsay and J. D. Read, "Psychotherapy and Memories of Childhood Sexual Abuse: A Cognitive Perspective," *Applied Cognitive Psychology* 8 (1994): 281–338.

On the role of "false beliefs" see Stephen J. Ceci, "False Beliefs:

Some Developmental and Clinical Considerations," in *Memory Distortion*, ed. Schacter, 91–125. Loftus and Ketcham, in *The Myth of Repressed Memory*, 275, cite George Ganaway, who writes even-handedly: "Psychotherapists and others are currently involved in the argument over the existence of 'robust repression'—whether an individual can keep extensive, important, personal information outside of conscious awareness for years, only to retrieve it later during therapy sessions. Assuming our patients are not consciously lying when they say they are not 'making up' their memories—and I have rarely found them to be lying—then, in fact, pseudomemories could not be created *without* a mechanism such as repression, or dissociation. Confabulated memories come to conscious awareness in such an effortless manner, especially while in trance, that they seem always to have been there, waiting to be 'discovered.' This may fool the patient and therapist alike. There must be some unconscious or 'repressed' organizing factor that strings together these bits and pieces of fact and fantasy in order to present the unconscious mind with such a convincing scenario."

3. There seems to be little evidence to support the claim that individuals forget cases of abuse that occur persistently over time, what has been referred to as "robust repression." The empirical evidence does not support claims for total amnesia in these cases. This has been a central claim of Frederick Crews, who in *The Memory Wars: Freud's Legacy in Dispute* (New York: New York Review of Books, 1995) provides a compelling argument refuting claims of total amnesia of gross abuse that occurs repeatedly over long periods of time. But in his interest in throwing out the baby of "robust repression" he makes a polemically compelling case— but scientifically unsupported one—against the bath water, that is, the very idea of repression *and* a psychodynamic theory upon which it is based. Instead, he associates himself with empirical research that identifies the powerful role of suggestion in "memory recovery." See, e.g., Michael Yapko, *Suggestions of Abuse: True and False Memories of Childhood Sexual Trauma* (New York: Simon

and Schuster, 1994). On the role played by the "retrieval environment" in memory recall, see, e.g., E. Tulving, *Elements of Episodic Memory* (Oxford: Clarendon Press, 1983); E. F. Loftus, *Eyewitness Testimony* (Cambridge, Mass.: Harvard University Press, 1979); D. P. Spence, "Narrative Truth and Putative Child Abuse," *International Journal of Clinical and Experimental Hypnosis* 42 (1994): 289–303.

4. Stolorow and Atwood, *Contexts of Being*, 18.

5. Anthony Giddens, "Action, Subjectivity and the Constitution of Meaning," *Social Research* 53 (1986): 533.

6. Jessica Benjamin has pioneered a "Hegelian" psychoanalysis, employing intersubjectivity to analyze human relationships and social pathologies. See, e.g., *The Bonds of Love: Psychoanalysis, Feminism, and the Problem of Domination* (New York: Pantheon, 1988); "An Outline of Intersubjectivity: The Development of Recognition," *Psychoanalytic Psychology* 7 (1990 supp.): 33–46; "Recognition and Destruction: An Outline of Intersubjectivity," in *Like Subjects, Love Objects: Essays on Recognition and Sexual Difference* (New Haven: Yale University Press, 1995).

7. Edward Hundert, *Philosophy, Psychiatry, and Neuroscience: Three Approaches to the Mind* (Oxford: Clarendon Press, 1989), 42.

8. Richard Terdiman, *Present Past: Modernity and the Memory Crisis* (Ithaca: Cornell University Press, 1993), 20–21.

9. Jerrold Seigel, "Hegel: Philosophy, Dialectic and Fate," in *Marx's Fate: The Shape of a Life* (Princeton: Princeton University Press, 1978), 19. Seigel offers a cogent discussion of Hegel's developmental psychology. My discussion of Hegel is indebted to Seigel.

10. Ibid., 16, 17. Seigel quotes from Hegel, *Encyclopedia of the Philosophical Sciences* (1830), trans. William Wallace, 131, 128.

11. Ibid., 63–64.

12. Hundert, *Philosophy, Psychiatry, and Neuroscience*, 43.

13. Karl Marx, "Alienated Labour," first manuscript of the *Economic and Philosophical Manuscripts*, trans. and ed. Tom Bottomore (New York: McGraw-Hill, 1963), 122.

14. Ibid., 124.

15. Ibid., 129. In these early writings Marx insists on alienation as part of the human condition, as part of the dialectic of history: it is the natural activity of men to produce their own alienation. In a challenging passage from "Alienated Labour" that reveals the enduring influence of Hegel, Marx makes this point and thereby demonstrates his conviction that the meaningful actions of individuals have created an external world that only *appears* as if it determines the nature and character of subjectivity: "The analysis of this concept [the movement of private property] shows that although private property appears to be the basis and cause of alienated labour, it is rather a consequence of the latter, just as the gods are *fundamentally* not the cause but the product of confusions of human reason. At a later stage, however, there is a reciprocal influence." Ibid., 131.

16. Stolorow and Atwood, *Contexts of Being*, 7–12.

17. Ibid., 10–11.

18. Ibid.; Marx and Engels, *Manifesto of the Communist Party,* in *The Marx-Engels Reader,* ed. Robert C. Tucker, 2d ed. (New York: Norton, 1978), 476. Stolorow and Atwood's characterization of alienation is clearly indebted to the Hegelian-Marxist analysis of intersubjectivity. They argue that psychological life is intersubjective, and they demonstrate the deleterious consequences when intersubjectivity is insufficiently emphasized in therapeutic settings. Their work is an important contribution to the current assault on the conception of the isolated individual. Stolorow and Atwood's insistence that the "myth" of the isolated individual is responsible for alienation is far different from Marx's consideration of the practices of social life that promote alienation: for Marx, the problem of alienation is more than misperception. It is a set of social arrangements that establish the isolated individual.

19. The work of the sociologist Pierre Bourdieu is relevant here. His lifelong project has been to overcome the dualism of subjectivity and objectivity in theorizing social life. He proposes

the concept of *habitus* to describe the practical life of social actors who have incorporated the social world "as a system of cognitive and motivating structures." These structures dispose actors to act in socially meaningful ways. Through individual agency, the social world is made and remade. Bourdieu locates cognition and motivation within an embedded social world but one that manifests itself through personal agency. *The Logic of Practice* (Stanford: Stanford University Press, 1990), 53.

20. Charles Taylor, *Philosophical Arguments* (Cambridge, Mass.: Harvard University Press, 1995), 171.

21. Robert Jay Lifton, *The Protean Self: Human Resilience in an Age of Fragmentation* (New York: Basic Books, 1993), 2, 28, 51.

22. Ibid., 28–29.

23. M. Merleau-Ponty, "The Body in Its Sexual Being," in Merleau-Ponty, *The Phenomenology of Perception*, trans. Colin Smith (London: Routledge and Kegan Paul, 1962), 154.

24. Ibid., 161, 166.

25. On unrepresented affective states, see Charles Spezzano, *Affect in Psychoanalysis: A Clinical Synthesis* (Hillsdale, N.J.: Analytic Press, 1993), 224–226.

26. Nancy Chodorow, *The Reproduction of Mothering: Psychoanalysis and the Sociology of Gender* (Berkeley and Los Angeles: University of California Press, 1978), 7.

27. Philippe Van Haute, "Fatal Attraction: Jean Laplanche on Sexuality, Subjectivity and Singularity in the Work of Sigmund Freud," *Radical Philosophy* 73 (1995): 8.

28. D. W. Winnicott, "Transitional Objects and Transitional Phenomena" (1953) in Winnicott, *Playing and Reality* (New York: Basic Books, 1971), 24.

29. Ibid., 9–10.

30. Ibid., 12.

31. Anthony Elliott, *Psychoanalytic Theory: An Introduction* (New York: Basil Blackwell, 1944), 25.

32. Christopher Bollas, *Being a Character: Psychoanalysis and Self-Experience* (New York: Hill and Wang, 1992), 30.

33. This structuring self, the self-in-formation, is a theme carried forward after Winnicott by the American psychoanalyst and self psychologist Heinz Kohut. Like Winnicott, Kohut adopts an intersubjective position in his understanding of psychopathology. He introduces a consideration of the consequence for psychopathology of "inadequate empathic attunement," that is, the incapacity of significant caregivers to respond to the developmental needs of the child. A failure to mirror the needs of a child, he argues, can render the child incapable of developing necessary self-structures. Heinz Kohut, *The Analysis of the Self* (Madison, Conn.: International Universities Press, 1971), 79.

34. Kurt W. Fischer and Catherine Ayoub, "Affective Splitting and Dissociation in Normal and Maltreated Children: Developmental Pathways for Self in Relationships," in D. Cicchetti and S. Toth, eds., *Rochester Symposium on Developmental Psychopathology,* vol. 5: *Dysfunctions of the Self* (Rochester, N.Y.: University of Rochester Press, 1994), 176.

35. Bollas, *Being a Character,* 58–59.

36. Karl Popper and John Eccles, *The Self and Its Brain* (New York: Springer-Verlag, 1981), 110–111.

37. Israel Rosenfield, *The Strange, Familiar and Forgotten: An Anatomy of Consciousness* (New York: Vintage, 1993), 8.

38. Nicholas Humphrey and Daniel Dennett, "Speaking for Ourselves: An Assessment of Multiple Personality Disorder," *Raritan* 9 (1989), 76, 80. Lifton, *The Protean Self,* 30.

39. Gilles Deleuze, *Empiricism and Subjectivity: An Essay on Hume's Theory of Human Nature* (New York: Columbia University Press, 1991), 86. Bollas, *Being a Character,* 27.

40. Terdiman, *Present Past,* 15.

4. Trauma and the Memory Wars

1. Cathy Caruth, "Introduction," in *Trauma: Explorations in Memory,* ed. Caruth (Baltimore: Johns Hopkins University Press, 1995), 1.

2. Eve Carlson and Judith Armstrong, "The Diagnosis and Assessment of Dissociative Disorders," in *Dissociation: Clinical and Theoretical Perspectives,* ed. J. Lynn and J. Rhue (New York: Guilford Press, 1994), 159; Eugene Bliss and Alan Jeppsen, "Prevalence of Multiple Personality among Inpatients and Outpatients," *American Journal of Psychiatry* 142 (1985): 250; Colin Ross et al., "The Frequency of Multiple Personality Disorder among Psychiatric Inpatients," *American Journal of Psychiatry* 148 (1991): 1717–20.

3. Nicholas Humphrey and Daniel Dennett, "Speaking for Ourselves: An Assessment of Multiple Personality Disorder," *Raritan* 9 (1989): 68–98. Nicholas Spanos, *Multiple Identities and False Memories: A Sociocognitive Perspective* (Washington: American Psychological Association, 1996), 2.

4. Caruth, *Trauma,* 5.

5. Elaine Showalter, *Hystories: Hysterical Epidemics and Modern Media* (New York: Columbia University Press, 1997), 6. Robert M. Woolsey, "Hysteria: 1875 to 1975," *Diseases of the Nervous System* 37 (July 1976): 379.

6. Mieke Bal, "Narrative Subjectivity," in *On Story-Telling: Essays in Narratology,* ed. David Jobling (Sonoma, Calif.: Polebridge Press, 1971), 147–148; see also George Dimock, "Anna and the Wolf-Man: Rewriting Freud's Case History," *Representations* 50 (1995): 73n.

7. Ian Hacking, *Rewriting the Soul: Multiple Personality and the Sciences of Memory* (Princeton: Princeton University Press, 1995), 86, 94. See also G. K. Ganaway, "Hypnosis, Childhood Trauma, and Dissociative Identity Disorder," *International Journal of Clinical and Experimental Hypnosis: Toward an Integrative Theory* 43 (1995): 127–144; Nicholas P. Spanos, "Child Abuse and Multiple Personality Disorder," in Spanos, *Multiple Identities and False Memories: A Sociocognitive Perspective* (Washington: American Psychological Association, 1996).

8. Hacking, *Rewriting the Soul,* 85, 93; emphasis added.

9. Ian Hacking, "World-Making by Kind-Making: Child Abuse

for Example," in *How Classification Works: Nelson Goodman among the Social Sciences*, ed. M. Douglas and D. Hull (Edinburgh: Edinburgh University Press, 1992), 180–238.

10. Judith Lewis Herman, *Trauma and Recovery* (New York: Basic Books, 1992), 57.

11. Hacking, *Rewriting the Soul*, 137.

12. Jeffrey Masson, *The Assault on Truth: Freud's Suppression of the Seduction Theory* (New York: Farrar, Straus and Giroux, 1984), 185.

13. Ibid., 185.

14. Bessel A. Van der Kolk and Onno Van der Hart, "The Intrusive Past: The Flexibility of Memory and the Engraving of Trauma," in *Trauma*, ed. Caruth, 158.

15. Ibid., 159, 166, 176.

16. Ibid., 163, 176.

17. Steven Lynn and Michael Nash, in "Truth in Memory: Ramifications for Psychotherapy and Hypnotherapy," *American Journal of Clinical Hypnosis* 36 (1994): 194–208, caution against a too easy correspondence between hypnotic technique, memory recall, and the development of a life narrative. While they suggest that those engaged in hypnotherapy should not, in all cases, privilege memory as truth, they recognize that such a method is at the heart of hypnosis. They attempt to establish a viable conception of "pseudomemory"—an aspiration far more subversive of the method than they acknowledge.

18. Herman, *Trauma and Recovery*, 43.

19. David Spiegel, "Hypnosis, Dissociation, and Trauma," in *Repression and Dissociation*, ed. Jerome L. Singer (Chicago: University of Chicago Press, 1990), 127. On contemporary research on hypnosis as a therapeutic tool see Nicholas Spanos, *Multiple Identities and False Memories: A Sociocognitive Perspective* (Washington: American Psychological Association, 1996), 17–56. Ironically, although Janet defined mental health in terms of the ridding of the self of dissociative disorders, he was as interested in the positive role of "therapeutic forgetting" to achieve this end as he was in "recovered memory." Janet argued for the heuristic

benefit of offering an alternative narrative account, often through hypnotic suggestion, a technique different from an effort to have the patient reexperience the trauma itself as the original source of dissociative states. As Ruth Leys writes, Janet insisted that "what mattered in treatment was not the 'confession' of traumatic memory but its elimination" Ruth Leys, "Traumatic Cures: Shell Shock, Janet, and the Question of Memory," *Critical Inquiry* 20 (1994): 661.

Contemporary followers of Janet, particularly those who resurrect his work to challenge Freudian orthodoxy, fail to emphasize his relative lack of interest in the recovery of the "truth," and cite instead Freud's dictum that uncovering the truth is the vehicle to freedom. Ian Hacking writes: "Janet had no compunction about lying to his patients, and creating false memories through which they could deal with their distress. Truth was not, for him, an absolute value. For Freud it was. That is to say, he aimed at the true theory to which all else had to be subservient, and he believed his patients should confront themselves" Hacking, *Rewriting the Soul*, 196.

20. John Toews, "Historicizing Psychoanalysis: Freud in His Time and for Our Time," *Journal of Modern History* 63 (1991): 513.

21. Alexander Schusdek, "Freud's Seduction Theory: A Reconstruction," *Journal of the History of the Behavioural Sciences* 2 (1966): 161, 163.

22. M. B. MacMillan, "Freud's Expectations and the Childhood Seduction Theory," *Australian Journal of Psychology* 29 (1977): 226.

23. Ibid., 230.

24. This is Frederick Crews's rhetorical gambit. Finding much at fault in the recovered memory movement, he launches a broadside assault on Freud as the originator of the phenomenon. See Frederick Crews et al., *The Memory Wars: Freud's Legacy in Dispute* (New York: New York Review of Books, 1995); see also Jeffrey Prager, "On the Abuses of Freud: A Reply to Masson and Crews," in *Debating Gender, Debating Sexuality,* ed. Nikki Keddi (New York: New York University Press, 1996).

25. Hacking, *Rewriting the Soul,* 3.

26. Sigmund Freud, "The Aetiology of Hysteria," S.E. 3: 206–207.

27. Richard Wollheim, *Sigmund Freud* (New York: Cambridge University Press, 1971), 26.

28. Sigmund Freud, "Moses and Monotheism," S.E. 23: 67.

29. Ibid., 72–73.

30. Sigmund Freud, *Introductory Lectures on Psycho-analysis,* S.E. 16: 275. Leys, "Traumatic Cures," 632.

31. *Moses and Monotheism,* 74.

32. Sigmund Freud, *Project for a Scientific Psychology,* S.E. 1: 356.

33. Sigmund Freud, "Screen Memories," S.E. 3: 315, 321. Richard King, "Memory and Phantasy," *Modern Language Notes* 98 (1983): 1197, 1200.

34. *Notes upon a Case of Obsessional Neurosis,* S.E. 10: 206.

35. Ned Lukacher, *Primal Scenes: Literature, Philosophy, Psychoanalysis* (Ithaca: Cornell University Press, 1986), 57, 58.

36. Freud quoted in George Ganaway, "Transference and Countertransference Shaping Influences on Dissociative Syndrome," in *Dissociation: Clinical and Theoretical Perspectives,* ed. Steven Jay Lynn and Judith W. Rhue (New York: Guilford Press, 1994), 317.

37. Ibid.

38. "Remembering, Repeating, and Working-Through," S.E. 12: 148, 151.

39. Ibid., 154.

40. Ibid., 151. Sigmund Freud, "The Dynamics of Transference," S.E. 12, 108.

41. Arnold H. Modell, *Other Times, Other Realities: Toward a Theory of Psychoanalytic Treatment* (Cambridge, Mass.: Harvard University Press, 1990), 65.

42. Ibid., 86; emphasis in original.

43. Robyn Fivush, "The Social Construction of Personal Narratives," *Merrill-Palmer Quarterly* 37 (1991): 59–81.

44. Kenneth J. Gergen, "Mind, Text, and Society: Self-Memory in Social Context," in *The Remembering Self: Construction and Ac-*

curacy in the Self-Narrative, ed. Ulric Neisser and Robyn Fivush (Cambridge: Cambridge University Press, 1994).

45. Donald P. Spence, *Narrative Truth and Historical Truth: Meaning and Interpretation in Psychoanalysis* (New York: Norton, 1982); see also Roy Schafer, *Retelling a Life: Narration and Dialogue in Psychoanalysis* (New York: Basic Books, 1992). Gergen, "Mind, Text, and Society," 164; emphasis in original.

46. Mikkel Borch-Jacobsen, "Hypnosis in Psychoanalysis," in Borch-Jacobsen, *The Emotional Tie: Psychoanalysis, Mimesis and Affect* (Stanford: Stanford University Press, 1993), 39–61.

47. "From the History of an Infantile Neurosis," S.E. 17: 51.

48. Lukacher, *Primal Scenes,* 140–141.

49. S.E. 17: 57.

50. Ruth Leys, "Death Masks: Kardiner and Ferenczi on Psychic Trauma," *Representations* 53 (1996): 60.

51. Once again, Freud may have not well executed clinically what he provided for metapsychologically. As Leys (ibid.) makes clear, Freud's uncertainty about trauma and its relation to his libidinal theory may have led him to overemphasize historical reconstruction and to underemphasize trauma's expression in the transference. This apparently was the case in his treatment of Abraham Kardiner, who, as Kardiner presents it, was traumatized by Freud and his interventions, a feature of the analysis that went unexplored as Freud earnestly worked on reconstructing Kardiner's traumatic past.

52. Caruth, "Introduction," in *Trauma,* ed. Caruth, 8–9, 4–5; emphasis in original. Leys, "Death Masks," 57.

53. D. W. Winnicott, "The Concept of Trauma in Relation to the Development of the Individual within the Family" (1965), in Winnicott, *Psycho-Analytic Explorations,* ed. Clare Winnicott, Ray Shepherd, and Madeleine Davis (Cambridge, Mass.: Harvard University Press, 1989). Quotation from "The Theory of the Parent-Infant Relationship," in Winnicott, *The Maturational Processes and the Facilitating Environment* (New York: International Universities Press, 1968), 37.

5. Toward an Intersubjective Science of Memory

1. For an excellent recent presentation of various approaches to the study of memory and memory distortion, see *Memory Distortion: How Minds, Brains, and Societies Reconstruct the Past,* ed. Daniel L. Schacter (Cambridge, Mass.: Harvard University Press, 1995). See also C. Brooks Brenneis, *Recovered Memories of Trauma: Transferring the Present to the Past* (Madison, Conn.: International Universities Press, 1997); Mark Pendergrast, "The Memory Maze," in *Victims of Memory: Sex Abuse Accusations and Shattered Lives,* 2d ed. (Hinesburg, Vt.: Upper Access Books, 1996); Jennifer J. Freyd, *Betrayal Trauma: The Logic of Forgetting Childhood Abuse* (Cambridge, Mass.: Harvard University Press, 1996). These references run the gamut from highly technical scientific presentations of research findings to more popular summaries and interpretations of memory studies. With the exception of Freyd, all the authors adopt the position that the phenomenon of recovered memory of gross abuse is a form of confabulation. Freyd cites evidence supportive of the claims of those who believe in the capacity of the mind to repress, and later to recover, horrible traumatic experience. Taken together these books document the polarization that exists and the capacity to invoke conventional science to buttress contending political stances on the controversy.

2. Antonio R. Damasio, *Descartes' Error: Emotion, Reason, and the Human Brain* (New York: Putnam, 1994), 226. For mind as a function of brain activity see, e.g., John Searles, "Minds and Brains without Programs," in *Mindwaves: Thoughts on Intelligence, Identity, and Consciousness,* ed. Colin Blakemore and Susan Greenfield (Oxford: Basil Blackwell, 1987): "Mental phenomena, whether conscious or unconscious, whether visual or auditory, pains, tickles, itches, thoughts, and all the rest of our mental life, are caused by processes going on in the brain. Mental phenomena are as much a result of electrochemical processes in the brain as digestion is a result of chemical processes going on in the stom-

ach" (220). And: "The intrinsically mental features of the universe are just higher-level features of brains" (224). In contrast with Damasio, who is interested in exploring subjectivity's unique configuration (resisting reductionism) and the mechanisms by which neuronal activity gives rise to conscious events, Searles insists that subjectivity "is an objective physical fact of biology" (226). "Brains cause minds," Searles writes (231).

3. Damasio, *Descartes' Error,* 226.

4. Ibid.; emphasis in original.

5. Ibid., 97.

6. Ibid., 98; emphasis in original.

7. Damasio illustrates this connection between thought and lower-order brain mechanisms with the following example: "If you have a dispositional representation for the face of Aunt Maggie, that representation contains not her face as such, but rather the firing patterns which trigger the momentary reconstruction of an approximate representation of Aunt Maggie's face, in early visual cortices. The several dispositional representations that would need to fire back, more or less synchronously, for Aunt Maggie's face to show up in the scopes of your mind, are located in several visual and higher-order association cortices (mostly, I suspect, in occipital and temporal regions). The same arrangement would apply in the auditory realm. There are dispositional representations for Aunt Maggie's voice in auditory association cortices, which can fire back to early auditory cortices and generate momentarily the approximate representation of Aunt Maggie's voice. There is not just one hidden formula for this reconstruction. Aunt Maggie as a complete person does not exist in one single site of your brain. She is distributed all over it, in the form of many dispositional representations, for this and that. And when you conjure up remembrances of things Maggie, and she surfaces in various early cortices (visual, auditory, and so on) in topographic representation, she is still present only in separate views during the time window in which you construct *some* meaning of her person" (ibid., 102–103; emphasis in original).

8. Ibid., 102, 104–105. Damasio distinguishes between innate knowledge and acquired knowledge. The former are typically somaticized and are "commands about biological regulation which are required for survival (e.g. the control of metabolism, drives, and instincts)." Innate knowledge typically does not manifest itself as images in the mind. We might describe it as "pre-objective." Acquired knowledge relies on more complex brain processes and may "contain records for the imageable knowledge that we can recall and which is used for movement, reason, planning, creativity. Acquired knowledge contains records of rules and strategies with which we operate on those images" (104–105). For my purposes, the critical feature of Damasio's argument lies, first, in specifying the different kinds of knowledge the mind possesses and, second, in specifying the way in which memory constitutes one dispositional form of the mind's practice of doing a learned, experiential "reading" of its own body and its own environment.

9. Hans Loewald, "Perspectives on Memory," in Loewald, *Papers on Psychoanalysis* (New Haven: Yale University Press, 1980), 150; emphasis added.

10. Ibid., 154, 155. For psychoanalysis's original statement situating perception in a complex personal environment, see one of Freud's prepsychoanalytic writings, *On Aphasia* (New York: International Universities Press, 1953), in which he was already exploding scientific orthodoxy.

11. Freud, *The Ego and the Id*, S.E. 19: 25–26; *Negation*, S.E. 19: 237–238; emphasis in original. Arnold Modell makes a similar point in commenting on the psychoanalytic transference relationship. Transference and transference-like experiences can be understood, he writes, as "a refinding in the present of a category from the past which may or may not prove to be a categorical fit; it is the imposition of an internal template upon what is presented from without." Modell, *Other Times, Other Realities* (Cambridge, Mass.: Harvard University Press, 1990), 65.

12. Loewald, "Perspectives on Memory," 157.

13. R. M. Dawes, "Biases of Retrospection," *Issues in Child Abuse Accusations* 1 (1991): 25–28. G. B. Marcus, "Stability and Change in Political Attitudes: Observe, Recall, and 'Explain,' " *Political Behavior* 8 (1986): 21–44. E. Eich, J. L. Reeves, B. Jaeger, and S. B. Graff-Radford, "Memory for Pain: Relation between Past and Present Pain Intensity," *Pain* 23 (1985): 375–379; P. M. Lewinsohn and M. Rosenbaum, "Recall of Parental Behavior by Acute Depressives, Remitted Depressives, and Nondepressives," *Journal of Personality and Social Psychology* 52 (1987): 611–619.

14. David Spiegel, "Hypnosis and Suggestion," in *Memory Distortion: How Minds, Brains and Societies Reconstruct the Past,* ed. Daniel L. Schacter (Cambridge, Mass.: Harvard University Press, 1995), 129. Daniel L. Schacter, "Memory Distortion: History and Current Status," ibid., 17–18.

15. Damasio, *Descartes' Error,* 139, 155; emphasis in original. The *New York Times* quotes Damasio as follows: "While people use facts, logic and pure reasoning to make decisions, these inputs are not enough. Decisions are also influenced by what has happened to a person in previous situations." Damasio speculates that "stored emotional memories come percolating up through a circuit in the pre-frontal lobes, the region of the brain involved in decision making." He refers to these emotional memories that influence decisions as "gut feelings." Sandra Blakeslee, "In Work on Intuition, Gut Feelings Are Tracked to Source: The Brain," *New York Times,* March 4, 1997, B11.

16. Loewald, "Perspectives on Memory," 159, 160–161.

17. Modell, *Other Times, Other Realities,* 64, 65. Loewald, "Perspectives on Memory," 165.

18. Stuart Hampshire, "A Kind of Materialism," in Hampshire, *Freedom of Mind and Other Essays* (Princeton: Princeton University Press, 1971), 216–217. On psychoanalytic materialism see Richard Wollheim, "Psychology, Materialism, and the Special Case of Sexuality," in Wollheim, *The Mind and Its Depths* (Cambridge, Mass.: Harvard University Press, 1993), 79–90.

19. Damasio, *Descartes' Error,* 108.

20. Freud, in *The Ego and the Id*, S.E. 19: 26, comments: "We have evidence that even subtle and difficult intellectual operations which ordinarily require strenuous reflection can equally be carried out preconsciously and without coming into consciousness. Instances of this are quite incontestable; they may occur, for example during the state of sleep, as is shown when someone finds, immediately after waking, that he knows the solution to a difficult mathematical or other problem with which he had been wrestling in vain the day before." Freud insists on the link between thought and imagistic thinking, whether conscious or not. Similarly, Damasio describes the self-reports of mathematicians and physicists, including Albert Einstein, Benoit Mandelbrot, and Richard Feynman, each depicting their thinking as being in pictures, even when considering the most abstract phenomena. Damasio, *Descartes' Error*, 107.

21. Charles Taylor, "To Follow a Rule," in Taylor, *Philosophical Arguments* (Cambridge, Mass.: Harvard University Press, 1995), 170, 171. Consider how new experiences are often "coded" by earlier, already processed and assimilated, experience. When one meets a new person, one often has a kind of associative recall: "She reminds me of someone. Who is it?" Or when one visits a new place one often has the impulse to "contain" the experience by comparing the location to other places, other times.

22. Modell, *Other Times, Other Realities*, 64.

23. Daniel Dennett, "Our Vegetative Soul," *Times Literary Supplement*, Aug. 25, 1995, 4. The term "reactivity cascade" is Damasio's to describe the process by which the self responds to disjunctures of experience. But Dennett, resisting an impulse to conceptualize a self as independent of the processes that create it, offers what he calls "a friendly amendment" to Damasio's formulation. He attempts to understand the activity of the self not as standing independent of the mind and body but as a product of a mind and body embedded in the social environment.

24. Hampshire, "A Kind of Materialism," 222. Leslie Brothers, *Friday's Footprint: How Society Shapes the Human Mind* (New York:

Oxford University Press, 1997), 118, 123. Brothers develops her intersubjective understanding of emotions: "The traditional emotion concept . . . should be replaced by the notion of a communicative loop of signaling and response. The sender of a signal— for example, a facial expression of knitted brows and bared teeth—triggers a complementary state in the receiver that causes, through evolutionarily inscribed pathways, a state of 'being threatened.' This state consists of complex bodily dispositions to act, such as release of fight-or-flight hormones, changes in blood pressure, cringing, and so on. 'Anger' and 'submissive fear' are two complementary behaviors, one of which triggers the other— and the significance of the threatening expression is given by the bodily changes it evokes in its recipient" (123).

25. Ibid., 31.

26. Ibid., 14.

27. Leon Eisenberg, "The Social Construction of the Brain," *American Journal of Psychiatry* 152 (1995): 1568; The term "ontogenetic niche" is drawn from M. J. West and A. P. King, "Settling Nature and Nurture into an Ontogenetic Niche," *Developmental Psychobiology* 20 (1987): 549–562. A. J. DeCaspar and M. J. Spence, "Prenatal Maternal Speech Influences Newborns' Perceptions of Speech Sounds," *Infant Behavior and Development* 9 (1986): 133–150. J. Mehler, W. Jusczyk, and G. Lambertz, "A Precursor to Language Development in Young Infants," *Cognition* 29 (1988): 143–178. G. Dawson, "Frontal Lobe Activity and Affective Behavior of Infants of Mothers with Depressive Symptoms," *Child Development* 63 (1992): 725–737.

28. Daniel Stern, *The Interpersonal World of the Infant* (New York: Basic Books, 1985). See also Robert Emde, "The Prerepresentational Self and Its Affective Core," *Psychoanalytic Study of the Child* 38 (1983): 165–192; Beatrice Beebe, Frank Lachmann, and Joseph Jaffe, "Mother-Infant Interaction Structures and Presymbolic Self and Object Representations," *Psychoanalytic Dialogues* 7 (1997): 133–182.

29. See J. Singer and J. Fagen, "Negative Affect, Emotional

Expression, and Forgetting in Young Infants," *Developmental Psychology* 28 (1992): 48–57; E. Tronick, "Emotions and Emotional Communication in Infants," *American Psychologist* 44 (1989): 112–119.

30. Brothers, *Friday's Footprint*, 15. For a complementary approach to the topic see Steven Pinker, *The Language Instinct* (New York: Morrow, 1994).

31. Gerald Edelman, *Neural Darwinism* (New York: Basic Books, 1987).

32. Beebe, Lachmann, and Jaffe, "Mother-Infant Interaction Structures," 146.

33. Edelman, *Neural Darwinism*, 270. For an excellent summary of Edelman's contribution to understanding memory see Israel Rosenfield, "Neural Darwinism: A New Approach to Memory and Perception," *New York Review of Books*, Oct. 9, 1986, 21–27.

34. Sir Frederick Bartlett, *Remembering: A Study in Experimental and Social Psychology* (Cambridge: Cambridge University Press, 1954 [1932]), 213. Daniel Schacter, "Memory Distortion: History and Current Status," 9, notes that Bartlett derived the notion of *schema* from the neurologist Henry Head, who in 1926 referred to an "organized mental representation of one's body" and applied it to memory.

35. Bartlett, *Remembering*, 206–207.

36. Ernest Schachtel, "On Memory and Childhood Amnesia," in *Metamorphosis: On the Development of Affect, Perception, Attention and Memory* (New York: Basic Books, 1959), 298.

37. Ulric Neisser, "John Dean's Memory: A Case Study," *Cognition* 9 (1981): 1.

38. Ibid., 19, 20.

39. Brothers, *Friday's Footprint*, 102; see also Rom Harre, *Social Being*, 2d. ed. (Oxford: Basil Blackwell, 1993), esp. 11–33; Charles Taylor, *Sources of the Self: The Making of the Modern Identity* (Cambridge, Mass.: Harvard University Press, 1989).

40. George Herbert Mead, *Mind, Self and Society: From the Standpoint of a Social Behaviorist,* ed. Charles Morris (Chicago: University of Chicago Press, 1974); see also Ruth Leys, "Mead's Voices: Imitation as Foundation; or, The Struggle against Mimesis," *Critical Inquiry* 19 (1993): 277–307. Erving Goffman, *The Presentation of Self in Everyday Life* (Garden City, N.Y.: Doubleday Anchor, 1959), 253.

Conclusion

1. Friedrich Nietzsche, "On the Uses and Disadvantages of History for Life," in Nietzsche, *Untimely Meditations* (New York: Cambridge University Press, 1983), 86, 123; emphasis in original.

2. Charles Taylor, "To Follow a Rule," in Taylor, *Philosophical Arguments* (Cambridge, Mass.: Harvard University Press, 1995), 170. Taylor's argument is not unlike Jean-François Lyotard's in an article entitled "Can Thought Go on Without a Body?" in *Materialities of Communication,* ed. Hans Gumbrecht and K. Ludwig Pfeiffer (Stanford: Stanford University Press, 1994), 286–300.

3. Thomas Csordas, *The Sacred Self: A Cultural Phenomenology of Charismatic Healing* (Berkeley: University of California Press, 1994).

Acknowledgments

This book began as part of my studies at the Southern California Psychoanalytic Institute. I want to thank the Institute for the psychoanalytic training it provided, and for the patients who first came to consult me under its auspices. Many teachers and supervisors generously donated their time to my psychoanalytic education, and their dedication to psychoanalysis inspired my own commitment. I am especially pleased to acknowledge Peter Loewenberg, who has worked tirelessly over the years on behalf of psychoanalytic training for academic researchers. I would like to express particular thanks to Abraham Gottesman and John Peck for their support. I am also profoundly indebted to my patients, who provided the most direct insight and inspiration. Finally, Leonard Comess's contribution to this work is unique; only he knows how helpful he has been.

Many people read earlier drafts and offered critical reactions and support of many kinds. I would like to thank Joyce Appleby, Morris Eagle, Anthony Elliott, Saul Friedlander, Janet Hadda, Daniel Hayes, Stavros Karageorgis, Rachel Klein, Marion Lefebre, John Lithgow, Herbert Morris, Anne Paplau, Melvin Pollner, Robert Pynoos, Katarina Rice, Michael Rustin, Margaret Rustin, Carl Schorske, Jerrold

Siegel, David Silverman, Debora Silverman, Tziona Silverman, Donald Spence, Shelley Taylor, Joan Waugh, Scott Waugh, Robert Westman, Victor Wolfenstein, and Mary Yeager.

While writing the book I participated in the Center for the Study of Intersubjectivity, a part of the Southern California Psychoanalytic Institute. Joseph Natterson is the inspiration behind the Center and has played a critical role in ensuring the open and inquiring tone of the group. Through my involvement with this group my views on intersubjectivity have been defined and elaborated. The Center provided important opportunities to present my writing to receptive and thoughtful readers, and the spirit of friendliness and support was never lost. I thank Karen Beard, Franklin Dines, Ray Friedman, Robert Hill, Joseph Natterson, Peter Schou, and Wendy Smith for their contributions to the book.

Research and writing were supported by several grants from the UCLA Academic Senate and a year-long fellowship from the American Council of Learned Societies. The book would have been, at best, long delayed without this funding, and I am grateful to these sources.

I would also like to thank, at Harvard University Press, Angela von der Lippe for her initial interest in the book and Elizabeth Knoll for seeing it through to publication. Special thanks to Camille Smith, whose talents for clarity of thought and simplicity of expression made this book far more readable and, I believe, better.

To acknowledge the importance to this project of my wife, Debby, and my son, Daniel, somehow contains rather than captures their significance to me and my work. I choose, instead, to dedicate the book to them.

Index